N LITERACIES
n and Education in the Electronic Age
d *by Ilana Snyder*

AFRICAN AMERICAN LITERACIES
Elaine Richardson

LITERACY IN THE NEW MEDIA AGE
Gunther Kress

SITUATED LANGUAGE AND LEARNING
A Critique of Traditional Schooling
James Paul Gee

Editorial Board:

SITUATED LANGUAGE AND LEARNING

A critique of traditional schooling

James Paul Gee

Routledge
Taylor & Francis Group

NEW YORK AND LONDON

First published 2004 in the USA and Canada
by Routledge
270 Madison Ave, New York, NY 10016

Simultaneously published in the UK
by Routledge
2 Park Square, Milton Park, Abingdon, Oxon, OX14 4RN

Reprinted 2006 (twice), 2007 (twice), 2008

Routledge is an imprint of the Taylor & Francis Group, an informa business

© 2004 James Paul Gee

Typeset in Baskerville by
BOOK NOW Ltd
Printed and bound in Great Britain by
TJ International Ltd, Padstow, Cornwall

Library of Congress Cataloging in Publication Data
A catalog record for this book has been requested

British Library Cataloguing in Publication Data
A catalogue record for this book is available from the British Library

ISBN10: 0–415–31777–0 (hbk)
ISBN10: 0–415–31776–2 (pbk)

ISBN13: 978–0–415–31777–1 (hbk)
ISBN13: 978–0–415–31776–4 (pbk)

SITUATED LANGUAGE
AND LEARNING

"In this major new work, James Paul Gee brings an insightful and original perspective to issues of literate identities, language and power, situated cognition and the provision of meaningful learning opportunities . . . An important and challenging book that raises fundamental questions and demands to be read by all those committed to ensuring that curricula and pedagogy meet the complex and diverse needs of learners in the twenty-first century."

Jackie Marsh, University of Sheffield, UK

Why do poor and minority students under-perform in school? Do computer games help or hinder learning? What can new research in psychology teach our educational policy-makers? In this major new book, Gee tackles the "big ideas" about language, literacy and learning, putting forward an integrated theory that crosses disciplinary boundaries, and applying it to some of the very real problems that face educationalists today.

Situated Language and Learning looks at the specialist academic varieties of language that are used in disciplines such as mathematics and the sciences. It argues that the language acquisition process needed to learn these forms of language is not given enough attention by schools and that this places unfair demands on poor and minority students.

The book compares this with learning as a process outside the classroom, applying this idea to computer and video games and exploring the particular processes of learning which take place as a child interacts with others and with technology to learn and play. In doing so, Gee examines what video games can teach us about how to improve learning in schools and engages with current debates on subjects such as "communities of practice" and "digital literacies."

Bringing together the latest research from a number of disciplines, *Situated Language and Learning* is a bold and controversial book by a leading figure in the field, and is essential reading for anyone interested in education and language.

James Paul Gee is the Tashia Morgridge Professor of Reading at the University of Wisconsin at Madison, USA. His previous publications include *Social Linguistics and Literacies* (Taylor & Francis 1996, 2nd edition), *An Introduction to Discourse Analysis* (Routledge 1999), and *What Video Games Have to Teach Us About Learning and Literacy* (2003).

LITERACIES
Series Editor: David Barton
Lancaster University

Literacy practices are changing rapidly in contemporary society in response to broad social, economic and technological changes: in education, the workplace, the media and in everyday life. The *Literacies* series has been developed to reflect the burgeoning research and scholarship in the field of literacy studies and its increasingly interdisciplinary nature. The series aims to situate reading and writing within its broader institutional contexts where literacy is considered as a social practice. Work in this field has been developed and drawn together to provide books that are accessible, interdisciplinary and international in scope, covering a wide range of social and institutional contexts.

CITY LITERACIES
Learning to Read Across Generations and Cultures
Eve Gregory and Ann Williams

LITERACY AND DEVELOPMENT
Ethnographic Perspectives
Edited by Brian V. Street

SITUATED LITERACIES
Theorising Reading and Writing in Context
Edited by David Barton, Mary Hamilton and Roz Ivanic

MULTILITERACIES
Literacy Learning and the Design of Social Futures
Edited by Bill Cope and Mary Kalantzis

GLOBAL LITERACIES AND THE WORLD-WIDE WEB
Edited by Gail E. Hawisher and Cynthia L. Selfe

STUDENT WRITING
Access, Regulation, Desire
Theresa M. Lillis

CONTENTS

CONTENTS

1

INTRODUCTION

I am a linguist whose interests have changed over the years. Today I am interested in the role language plays in learning. However, earlier in my career I spent my time studying things like "naked infinitives." This is, of course, a topic that sounds a lot sexier than it is. Naked infinitives are grammatical constructions like the verb "leave" in "I saw Mary leave." In this sentence, "leave" is an "infinitive" (a verb not marked for "tense," that is not marked as "present" or "past"). In English, infinitives are usually preceded by a "to," as in "I wanted Mary to leave." Since the "to" is missing in "I saw Mary leave," "leave" is said to be "naked." I also studied "headless relatives," another topic that sounds more exciting than it is. Headless relatives are grammatical constructions like "who I want to marry" in "I will marry who I want to marry." "Who I want to marry" is a relative clause. Such clauses are normally preceded by a noun phrase called their "head," as in "I will marry the person I want to marry," where "the person" is the head of the relative clause. Thus, since there is no head in front of "who I want to marry" in "I will marry who I want to marry," it is called a "headless relative clause."

This book has nothing to do with naked infinitives or headless relatives. It does, however, have something to do with why the last paragraph, my first in the book, will not be very inviting to many readers. You don't really want to hear a lot more technical information about naked infinitives and headless relatives, do you? You lost a lot of your interest when you found out naked infinitives had nothing to do with naked bodies and headless relatives had nothing to do with decapitating people. If you didn't like school, the first paragraph reminded you a lot of school, except that school didn't even try to titillate you with nakedness and decapitation.

For some people the first paragraph was alienating, for others it wasn't. Some feared I would continue, perhaps to do something like tell them what parasitic gaps are. Some few might have hoped I would continue – too few to sell enough copies of this book to keep me alive. People who found the first paragraph alienating feared they were about to fall into the black hole of "jargon" and "academic language" – language they don't particularly like or care about. It's a black hole they experienced too often in school. On the other hand, people who can't wait for the parasitic gap discussion have, for one reason or another, made a larger peace with academic ways with words.

In the not too distant past people who had made peace with school-based academic jargon and ways with words could be pretty much assured, all things being equal, of success in modern developed countries. But the times they are a-changing and things are more problematic now. Today, to hedge your bets, you probably want to make some sort of peace with academic learning – with school-based learning. But there are new ways with words, and new ways of learning, afoot in the world – ways not necessarily connected to academics or schools. These ways are, in their own fashion, just as special, technical, and complex as academic and school ways. But they are motivating for many people for whom school wasn't. At the same time, they may be alienating for many people for whom school ways were motivating. These new ways, though, are just as impor-tant – maybe more important – for success in the modern world as school ways. These new ways are the ways with words (and their concomitant ways of think-ing) connected to contemporary digital technologies and the myriad of popular culture and specialist practices to which they have given rise.

We face, then, a new challenge: how to get all children – rich and poor – to be successful in school, but to ensure also that all children – rich and poor – are able to learn, think, and act in new ways fit for our new high-tech global world. We have barely begun on the first task only to have the second become more pressing by the day.

Most of you will be glad to know that I don't do theoretical linguistics any more. I have for the last number of years been an educational linguist, interested in how language and learning work at school and in society at large. But, alas, some of you will find that I still write in "jargon" and academic language. Others will find my writing a bit too "folksy" – not academic enough for rigorous reputability. It all depends on the sorts of peace you have or have not made with certain ways with words. I have tried to be as clear as I can while still using the language tools I need to get my job done – and that is part of the point of this book: that there are different ways with words because we need different tools to get different sorts of jobs done. More generally, this book is about the tension that we readers, former students all, feel about academic and school-based forms of language and thinking, that some people find alienating and others find liberating. It is about facing that tension at a time when these academic and school-based ways are challenged by new ways with words and new ways of thinking and learning.

This book will constantly move back and forth between ways with words, deeds, and thoughts in school and out of school. Predominant among the out-of-school things I talk about will be computer and video games (I will in this book just use the term "video games" to mean both computer and video games). Some of my most academic readers will now themselves fear a black hole, in this case a place where they haven't been and don't want to be. I hope I can convince such readers that this is a mistake. For many people in our modern world – not all of them particularly young – video games are not a black hole, but a liberating entrée to new worlds – worlds more compelling than either the worlds they see or have seen at school or read about in academic books. But, then, the core argument of this book will be that people learn new ways with words, in or out of school, only when they find the worlds to which these words apply compelling.

This book is actually one argument, broken into pieces, that can be summarized fairly concisely. So here is a quick overview of what is to come:

1 What's hard about school is not learning to read, which has received the lion's share of attention from educators and policy-makers, but learning to read and learn in academic content areas like mathematics, social studies, and science (students can't get out of a good high school, let alone get out of any decent college, if they can't handle their content-area textbooks in biology or algebra). Unfortunately, a good many students, at all levels of schooling, hate the types of language associated with academic content areas. Indeed, many people in the public don't very much like us academics and our "ways with words."

2 What's hard about learning in academic content areas is that each area is tied to academic specialist varieties of language (and other special symbol systems) that are complex, technical, and initially alienating to many learners (just open a high-school biology or algebra textbook). These varieties of language are significantly different from people's "everyday" varieties of language, sometimes called their "vernacular" varieties.

3 Such academic varieties of language are integrally connected (actually "married") to complex and technical ways of thinking. They are the tools through which certain types of content (e.g. biology or social studies) are thought about and acted on.

4 Privileged children (children from well-off, educated homes) often get an important head start before school at home on the acquisition of such academic varieties of language; less privileged children (poor children or children from some minority groups) often do not. The privileged children continue to receive support outside of school on their academic language acquisition process throughout their school years, support that less privileged children do not receive.

5 Schools do a very poor job at teaching children academic varieties of language. Indeed, many schools are barely aware they exist, that they have to be learned, and that the acquisition process must start early. At best they believe you can teach children to think (e.g. about science or mathematics) without worrying too much about the tools children do or do not have with which to do that thinking. Indeed, schools create more alienation over academic varieties of language and thinking than they do understanding.

6 All children, privileged and not, can readily learn specialist varieties of language and their concomitant ways of thinking as part and parcel of their "popular culture." These specialist language varieties are, in their own ways,

3

as complex as academic varieties of language. The examples I use in the book involve Pokémon and video games. (If you don't think things like Pokémon involve specialist language and ways of thinking connected to it, go get some Pokémon or Digimon cards.) There are many more such examples. While confronting specialist academic languages and thinking in school is alienating, confronting non-academic specialist languages and thinking outside school often is not.

7 The human mind works best when it can build and run simulations of experiences its owner has had (much like playing a video game in the mind) in order to understand new things and get ready for action in the world. Think about an employee role-playing a coming confrontation with a boss, a young person role-playing an imminent encounter with someone he or she wants to invite out on a date, or a soldier role-playing his or her part in a looming battle. Such role-playing in our minds helps us to think about what we are about to do and usually helps us to do it better. Think about how poorly such things go when you have had no prior experiences with which to build such role-playing simulations and you have to go in completely "cold." Furthermore, a lecture on employee–employer relations, dating, or war won't help anywhere near as much as some rich experiences with which you can build and run different simulations to get ready for different eventualities.

8 People learn (academic or non-academic) specialist languages and their concomitant ways of thinking best when they can tie the words and structures of those languages to experiences they have had – experiences with which they can build simulations to prepare themselves for action in the domains in which the specialist language is used (e.g. biology or video games).

9 Because video games (which are often long, complex, and difficult) are simulations of experience and new worlds, and thus not unlike a favored form of human thinking, and because their makers would go broke if no one could learn to play them, they constitute an area where we have lots to learn about learning. Better yet, they are a domain where young people of all races and classes readily learn specialist varieties of language and ways of thinking without alienation. Thus it is useful to think about what they can teach us about how to make the learning of specialist varieties of language and thinking in school more equitable, less alienating, and more motivating.

10 In the midst of our new high-tech global economy, people are learning in new ways for new purposes. One important way is via specially designed spaces (physical and virtual) constructed to resource people tied together, not primarily via shared culture, gender, race, or class, but by a shared interest or endeavor. Schools are way behind in the construction of such spaces. Once again, popular culture is ahead here.

11 More and more in the modern world, if people are to be successful, they must become "shape-shifting portfolio people": that is, people who gain many diverse experiences that they can then use to transform and adapt themselves for fast-changing circumstances throughout their lives.

12 Learning academic varieties of language and thinking in school is now "old." It is (for most people) important, but not sufficient for success in modern society. People must be ready to learn new specialist varieties of language and thinking outside of school, not necessarily connected to academic disciplines, throughout their lives. Children are having more and more learning experiences outside of school that are more important for their futures than is much of the learning they do at school.

Well, let's jump in. I hope it's not a black hole for any of you.

2

A STRANGE FACT ABOUT NOT LEARNING TO READ

A strange fact

Politicians, policy-makers, and media in the United States claim we have a "reading crisis" (National Institute of Child Health and Human Development 2000a, b). They argue that lots of children are not learning to read well enough. Traditionalists argue that this is because children don't get enough overt instruction on "phonics": that is, the relationship between sounds and letters (e.g. the fact that the letter "a" stands for different sounds in words like "bat", "bate", and "calm"). More progressive educators argue it is because schools are too centered on meaningless and unmotivating skill-and-drill.

Oddly enough, learning to read is not a good thing over which to have a major controversy. Most children learn to read, regardless of what instructional approach a school adopts, as long it is not particularly stupid (Coles 1998, 2000). Furthermore, school children in the United States do well on international comparisons of early reading (Elley 1992; Snow *et al.* 1998).

Who, then, are the children who do not fare well in early reading? Some are children with genuine neurological disorders making learning to read quite difficult. But the majority are poor or come from minority groups whose members have faced a history of prejudice and oppression (Snow *et al.* 1998). Though this fact is now well known enough to be taken for granted, we ought to see it as strange. Why should being poor or a member of a particular social group have anything whatsoever to do with learning to read in school? Isn't the whole purpose of public schooling to create a level playing field for all children?

I should hasten to add that, though I will concentrate now on "poor" and minority children, the issue is not really poverty or minority group status in and of itself. The real issue is failing, for whatever reason, to be a member of a particular "in group." For now, let's just call this "in group" the "school club." You don't have to be particularly poor to fail to be a member of this "in group." You simply have to feel unaffiliated with school and formal schooling for any of a variety of reasons. Not everyone who goes to school is in the "school club" and not everyone who is not in the club is poor or non-white. But, for now, let's leave this issue aside and continue to talk about poverty and minority status.

Controversies over reading should have less to do with debates about methods of instruction and more to do with understanding the links between poverty and (not) learning to read. Understanding these links will illuminate much wider issues about learning and schooling, as well. The strange fact that poverty and learning to read in school are linked is not caused by poor children being less good at learning than rich kids. To see that this is so, consider the phenomenon of Pokémon, perhaps the longest-running popular culture "fad" ever (waning now, though the points made below could equally well be made with Digimon, Dragon Ball Z, or Yu-Gi-Oh). Pokémon ("Pocket Monsters") are odd-looking little creatures that human trainers care for. They can fight each other, but losers don't die, they just fall asleep. Pokémon appear on cards, as plastic figures, in video games, and in television shows and movies.

There are over 250 Pokémon now. But let's just consider the Pokémon world as of the time the Nintendo Game Boy games *Pokémon Red, Blue*, and *Yellow* were out in the late 1990s (e.g., see, Hollinger and Ratkos 1999). Newer games have introduced yet more Pokémon. At the time, there were 150 Pokémon. They all had polysyllabic names, ranging from Aerodactyle through Nidoran to Wartortle. Each Pokémon name stands not for just an individual Pokémon, but a type. A child can collect several Aerodactyles or Nidorans in a game.

Each Pokémon falls into one of 16 types (Bug, Dark, Dragon, Electric, Fighting, Fire, Ghost, Grass, Ground, Ice, Normal, Poison, Psychic, Rock, Steel, and Water) that determines how the Pokémon fights. There are actually more than 16 types, since some Pokémon are mixed or hybrid types, but let's leave that aside. Take Charmander, a Pokémon that looks something like an orange dinosaur with fire coming out of its long tail, as an example. Charmander is a Fire type and has such attack skills as Ember, Leer, Flamethrower, and Spin Fire.

Many, but not all, Pokémon can evolve, as they gain experience, into one or two other Pokémon. Thus, Charmander can evolve into Charmeleon. Charmander and Charmeleon look alike except that Charmeleon has horns. In turn, Charmeleon can eventually evolve into Charizard, who looks like Charmeleon with wings.

Each Pokémon has a set of skills that determines various sorts of attacks that the Pokémon can make in fights against other Pokémon. For example, Charmander has the following attack skills (some of which are obtained only when the player's Charmander advances to a certain skill level by winning battles in the game): Scratch, Growl, Ember, Leer, Rage, Slash, Flamethrower, and Fire Spin. Some Pokémon have a somewhat shorter list of attack skills, many have a longer list. Let's for simplicity's sake say that each Pokémon has eight possible attack skills.

There are other things children know about each Pokémon (e.g. which type is particularly good or bad at fighting which other types). But let's stop here. What does a child have to know to name and recognize Pokémon? The child has to learn a system: the Pokémon system. And that system is this: 150 Pokémon names; 16 types; 2 possible other Pokémon a given Pokémon can evolve into;

8 possible attack skills from a list of hundreds of possible skills. The system is 150 × 16 × 2 × 8, and, of course, we have greatly simplified the real system.

However, many children's Pokémon knowledge is deeper than even this implies. Children we have studied could readily name all 150 Pokémon and state their type, skills, and what other Pokémon they could evolve into when shown a picture of a Pokémon. But they could do more. When they searched for pictures of Pokémon on the Internet, the picture often came in slowly, one little strip at a time. When a small part of the top of a Pokémon was on the screen and the children were waiting for the rest of the picture to fill in, they could often identify the Pokémon. Since these children can identify one of 150 Pokémon by seeing only a small bit of it, this means that they have done a feature analysis of the whole system. From a small subset of one Pokémon's features, the child can discriminate that Pokémon from all the others.

We had no trouble finding children who knew their Pokémon – children as young as five and six. Some of these children did not yet play the Pokémon video games or the card game. They knew Pokémon as plastic figures and pictures from books and the Internet. They imagined and acted out their fights, based on what they had learned from "Pokedexes" they had seen in books or on the Internet (a "Pokedex" is a list of the Pokémon, their types, evolutionary states, and skills).

I know of no evidence that mastering the Pokémon universe differs by the race, class, and gender of children. Poor children do it as well as rich, if they have access to the cards, games, or figures. Many schools banned Pokémon cards because poor children couldn't get as many cards as richer children and spent lots of times trying to trade cards at recess. You can't make good trades if you don't know the system. There is no evidence that poor children weren't often sagacious traders. In fact, it seems a bit strange – creepy even – to claim that an African-American child or a poor child might be inherently less able to engage with Pokémon than white or rich children. We do not, however, find such thoughts strange when we think about school learning, though we should. Certainly the capitalists who made and sell Pokémon have more trust in non-white and poor children than that.

Now, consider the following paradox. Traditionalists claim that the big problem in our schools is that we need to teach "phonics skills" more overtly and intensively. Phonics is the mapping between sound and letters (the fact that the letter "a" sometimes makes the sound /ae/, in a word like "mat"; the sound /ah/, in a word like "calm"; and the sound /A/, in a word like "made"). When children have to learn phonics, they are faced with a system of 44 phonemes (the basic speech sounds in English) coupled with 26 letters of the alphabet. That is, the child needs to learn with which of 44 sounds each of 26 letters can be associated. This system is pitifully smaller than the Pokémon system. That system is 150 (Pokémon) coupled with 16 (types) coupled with 2 (evolutions) coupled with 8 (skills) Yet, in the case of learning to read at school, we need to spend billions of dollars on government-sponsored reading initiatives (like the No Child Left Behind legislation) to teach children to match these 44 phonemes and 26 letters.

Furthermore, in the case of learning to read in school, but not in the case of learning Pokémon, race and class make a big difference, since poor children and children from some minority groups, on average, learn to read in school less well than more privileged children.

Many people confronted with the Pokémon argument say something like this: "But Pokémon is entertaining and motivating. School can't compete with that." So are we to conclude that science, for instance, one of human beings' most spectacular achievements, is neither fun nor motivating? You won't get very far convincing any good scientist of this. But, be that as it may, the real problem is this: We all know that if we turned Pokémon into a subject on the school curriculum, then certain children, many of them poor, would all of a sudden have trouble learning Pokémon. This is not (yet or necessarily) a criticism. For now, it is just a fact.

So what is it about school that manages to transform children who are good at learning (witness Pokémon), regardless of their economic and cultural differences, into children who are not good at learning, if they are poor or members of certain minority groups?

Learning to read

In the debates over reading, traditionalists advocate a sequential, skills-based approach to reading instruction (Carnine *et al.* 1996; Lyon 1998; National Institute of Child Health and Human Development 2000a, b). It's all about "basic skills" (see Coles 1998, 2000, 2003 for discussion). First there is instruction on "phonemic awareness" (the conscious awareness that oral words are composed of individual sounds), then on phonics (matching letters to sounds), then practice with fluent oral reading (reading out loud), then work on comprehension skills. Each stage is supposed to guarantee the next. It's a virtual assembly line. Henry Ford would have been proud. Traditionalists argue that learning to read requires overt instruction. For them, reading is what we can call an "instructed process."

More progressive educators, on the other hand, stress meaning-making (Edelsky 1994). They believe that people learn to read best when they pick up the skills stressed by the traditionalists as part and parcel of attempting to give meaning to written texts. There have been many different non-traditionalist approaches, though Whole Language has been the best known of these after the 1950s (Goodman 1998). Traditionalists find the whole meaning-making argument romantic nonsense – a leftover 1960s permissive coddling of children.

Advocates of Whole Language argue that learning to read is a "natural" process in the same way in which the acquisition of one's native language is a natural process (see Cazden 1972: pp. 139–42 for early and critical discussion of the issue). Every human child, barring those with quite severe disorders, acquires his or her native language through immersion in talk and activity. No instruction is needed or helpful. Whole Language advocates argue that this is how children should acquire literacy as well.

Many linguists, following the work of Noam Chomsky (e.g. 1965, 1968, 1986, 1995; see also Pinker 1994), argue that the acquisition of one's native oral language happens in this "natural" way because acquiring a first language is biologically supported in human beings. Much as some species of birds know innately how to build their species-specific nest or sing their species-specific song, human children know innately what a human language can look like (including the parameters of possible variation across human languages) and how to go about "building" one. This is to say, in a sense, that for human beings acquiring a native language is a type of "instinct."

Today's reading traditionalists, supported by many linguists, myself included (Gee 2001; Rayner *et al.* 2001, 2002), argue that learning to read, unlike acquiring one's first oral language, cannot be a biologically supported process and, thus, cannot be "natural." Literacy (written language) is too new a process historically to have had the evolutionary time required to have become "wired" into our human genetic structure. Written language is, at the very best, 6000 to 10,000 years old – too short a time to have gained biological support. Furthermore, written language was invented by only a few cultures and only a few times, unlike oral language, which has existed for all human cultures for long enough to have become part of our human biological inheritance.

Learning to read is not a natural process like acquiring a first language or, for that matter, learning to walk. Such natural processes simply happen when a child is exposed to the right sorts of input and environments (e.g. speaking with others, moving around a 3D world). They "unfold." So does this mean, as the traditionalists argue, that reading is an instructed process? Does learning to read require lots of overt instruction? Not necessarily.

There are actually three major learning processes in human development, not two (natural and instructed). When humans acquire something by a natural process, like their first language or walking, we find that everyone, barring those with serious disorders, succeeds and succeeds well. This is the hallmark of biologically supported acquisition. All human beings acquire their first language well, and about equally well as everyone else (just the same happens with learning to walk). It never happens that Janie, a smart little girl, acquires English relative clauses, though Johnnie, a dumb little boy, acquires the rest of English but just can't get those pesky relative clauses. Of course people acquire different dialects depending on where they are born and into which cultural group.

There are many things that for most human beings are acquired by more or less overt instruction. This is how most people acquire knowledge of physics, social studies, and mathematics. In such cases, we humans have no support from our biological inheritance. Even when instruction is good, we find a pattern in such cases where a small number of people succeed quite well and a far greater number succeed much less well. Every human is built to learn a native language well; not everyone is built to learn physics well.

We can construe the traditionalists' argument that learning to read is an instructed process as a claim that learning to read is more like learning physics

11

than learning one's native oral language. We can construe the Whole Language argument that learning to read is a natural process as a claim that learning to read is more like learning one's native language than learning physics. They are both wrong, since learning to read is neither like learning one's native oral language nor like learning physics.

Besides natural and instructed learning processes, there are also what we can call "cultural processes." There are some things that are so important to a cultural group that the group ensures that everyone who needs to learns them (Lave and Wenger 1991; Rogoff 1990). Take cooking, for example. Human cultures have always ensured that people (or, perhaps, only certain people like, unfortunately, in some cultures, women) learn how to cook and cook well enough to keep themselves and others alive and well. Here we see a pattern where a few people really excel (as in physics), but everyone who needs to, again barring serious disorders, learns "well enough" (like acquiring a human language, though for cooking and other cultural achievements the standard of excellence need not be as high as speaking a native language). If most people learned to cook as well as they learn physics, whole cultures would starve.

How, for the most part, have people learned to cook in human cultures? Usually not via cooking classes. The process involves "masters" (adults, more masterful peers) creating an environment rich in support for learners. Learners observe masters at work. Masters model behavior (e.g. cooking a particular type of meal) accompanied by talk that helps learners know what to pay attention to. Learners collaborate in their initial efforts with the masters, who do most of the work and scaffold the learners' efforts. Texts or other artifacts (e.g. recipes, cookbooks) that carry useful information, though usually of the sort supplied "on demand" or "just in time" when needed, are often made available. The proper tools are made available as well, many of which carry "knowledge" learners need not store in their heads (e.g. pans made of certain materials "know" how to spread heat properly). Learners are given continual verbal and behavioral feedback for their efforts. And, finally, learners are aware that masters have a certain socially significant identity (here, "cook") that they wish to acquire as part and parcel of membership in a larger cultural group. In my view – and this will be a major theme of this book – this last point about identity is crucial.

Now here is a problem with what I have just said: cultural learning processes like learning to cook (or tell stories, give and get gifts, hunt, engage in warfare, set up a household) undoubtedly have their origin in the basic workings of human culture. However, long ago specific groups of human beings learned how to engage in this learning process even when they were not really "cultures" or were cultures only in some extended sense. For example, what I have called a cultural learning process is how the vast majority of young people today learn to play computer and video games (and the vast majority of them do play such games). People who play video games don't really constitute a "culture" in any classic anthropological sense, though we can certainly use the word in an extended sense here, at least for the time being.

12

Let us return for a moment to instructed processes. We have argued that for most people learning something like physics is an instructed process. However, physicists (masters of physics) long ago realized that if you want someone really to learn physics deeply in the sense of becoming a physicist then, sooner or later, you need to turn learning physics into a cultural and not an instructed process (or not just an instructed process). Why? Because it is clear that deep learning works better as a cultural process than it does as an instructed process. Most humans are not, in fact, very good at learning via overt instruction. For example, most young people would resist learning to play video games via lots of overt instruction – and for a good reason: instruction is a much less efficient process (in all sorts of ways) than learning to play video games via a cultural process (i.e. via becoming a member of the games culture).

What does it mean to learn physics as a cultural process (in our extended sense of "culture" where we are counting physicists as being their own cultural group)? Much the same as what it meant to learn cooking as a cultural process. Masters (physicists) allow learners to collaborate with them on projects that the learners could not carry out on their own. Learners work in a "smart" environment filled with tools and technologies, and artifacts store knowledge and skills they can draw on when they do not personally have such knowledge and skills. Information is given "just in time" when it can be put to use (and thus better understood) and "on demand" when learners feel they need it and can follow it. Extended information given out of a context of application (thus not "just in time") is offered after, not before, learners have had experiences relevant to what that information is about. Learners see learning physics as not just "getting a grade" or "doing school," but as part and parcel of taking on the emerging identity of being a physicist.

In today's schools many instructed processes, not least those connected to learning to read, involve practicing skills outside any contexts in which they are used by people who are adept at those skills (e.g. good readers). If this is how children had to learn to play a computer or video game – and, remember, these games are often very long and quite challenging – the games industry would go broke.

Children who learn to read successfully do so because, for them, learning to read is a cultural and not primarily an instructed process. Furthermore, this cultural process has long roots at home – roots which have grown strong and firm before the child has walked into a school. Children who must learn reading primarily as an instructed process in school are at an acute disadvantage. It would be like learning to cook or play video games via lectures or decontextualized skill-and-drill. Possible, maybe, but surely neither effective nor easy.

Let me add here too that as schools turn reading into an instructed process, today's children see more and more powerful instances of cultural learning in their everyday lives in things like Pokémon and video games. Modern high-tech society – thanks to its media, technology, and creative capitalists – gets better and better at creating powerful cultural learning processes. Schools do not.

Deep cause of reading failure

So the argument thus far is this: though you can turn learning to read into an instructed process, it works best as a cultural process. However, traditionalists would have us believe that poor readers, young and old, have failed to learn to read well because they have received poor skills instruction early on in school. In fact, this is the traditionalists' answer to everything: kids learn math and science and anything else poorly in school because they receive poor skills training. It's all about skills.

There is good reason, though, to believe that this traditionalist claim is not true, at least for people who do not have a genuine neurologically based reading disorder. Poor readers have not failed because of bad skills instruction, though, indeed, they may have received bad skills instruction. They have failed for a variety of more important reasons, one of which we will get to below (the others will have to wait until later chapters).

One skill that the contemporary traditionalists have focused on is "phonemic awareness." Phonemic awareness is the conscious awareness that oral words are composed of individual phonemes or "sounds." Thus, the word "shoe" is made up of two sounds, /sh/ and /u/, though the word happens to be spelled with four letters. Traditionalists now see phonemic awareness as the crucial prerequisite skill for learning to read (National Institute of Child Health and Human Development 2000a). And, indeed, non-literates often are unaware that oral words are made up of discrete sounds, though they are aware that words are composed of syllables. Thus, non-literates might not be aware that "mischief" has six sounds in it (/m/, /i/, /s/, /ch/, /i/, /f/), but they are aware that it can be decomposed into "mis" and "chief," though they need not know these things are called "syllables."

The central significance traditionalists place on phonemic awareness training is misplaced, though it is typical of traditionalists that they place great emphasis on skills outside the uses to which they are put. Consider, for example, the remarks below from the National Academy of Sciences' report *Preventing reading difficulties in young children* (Snow *et al.* 1998; in the quotes below, the term "phonological awareness" is used for phonemic awareness and other aspects of knowledge about how sound works in oral language):

> studies indicate that training in phonological awareness, particularly in association with instruction in letters and letter-sound relationships, makes a contribution to assisting at risk children in learning to read. The effects of training, although quite consistent, are only moderate in strength, and have so far not been shown to extend to comprehension. Typically a majority of the trained children narrow the gap between themselves and initially more advanced students in phonological awareness and word reading skills, but few are brought completely up to speed through training, and a few fail to show any gains at all.
>
> (p. 251)

While a stress on phonological awareness and overt phonics instruction does initially help "at risk" students, it does not bring them up to par with more advantaged students. In fact, they tend eventually to fall back, fueling the phenomenon known as the "fourth-grade slump" (this fact is amply documented in the report, see pp. 216, 228, 232, 248–9, 251, 257). The "fourth-grade slump" (Chall *et al.* 1990) is the phenomenon where some children seem to acquire reading (i.e. pass reading tests) fine in the early grades, but fail to be able to use reading to learn school content in the later grades, when the language demands of that content (e.g. science) get more and more complex. The fourth-grade slump is made up of kids who can "read," in the sense of decode and assign superficial literal meanings to texts, but can't "read" in the sense of understanding, in any deep way, informational texts written in fairly complex language.

From remarks like the one quoted above, it would certainly seem that the problems poor and minority children have with learning to read must lie, for the most part, someplace else than a lack of early phonemic awareness training or other early "basic skills" training. The fourth-grade slump tells us this much (because here we see kids who have mastered early reading skills of the sorts traditionalists stress, but still can't read to learn in the later grades). But what is the problem then?

Though *Preventing reading difficulties in young children* (Snow *et al.* 1998) is, by and large, a traditionalist document, the report acknowledges that there is something else that is more significant than early phonological awareness in predicting early success at learning to read. This is what the report calls "early language ability," a loaded phrase, indeed.

> Chaney (1992) also observed that performance on phonological aware-ness tasks by preschoolers was highly correlated with general language ability. Moreover it was measures of semantic and syntactic skills, rather than speech discrimination and articulation, that predicted phonological awareness differences.
>
> (p. 53)

> What is most striking about the results of the preceding studies is the power of early preschool language to predict reading three to five years later.
>
> (pp. 107–8)

Let's be clear: in the first quote above, "measures of semantic and syntactic skills" means how well children deal with what language means and with its structure ("syntax"). Kids who are good with meaning and structure in language also acquire good phonemic awareness early on and later learn to read well.

So what is this early language ability that seems so important for later success in school? According to the report, it is indicated by things like vocabulary (recep-tive vocabulary, but more especially expressive vocabulary, p. 107); the ability to recall and comprehend sentences and stories; and the ability to engage in extended, connected verbal interactions on a single topic. Furthermore, I think that research has made it fairly clear what causes such language ability. What appears to cause it are family, community, and school language environments in which children interact intensively with adults and more advanced peers and experience cognitively challenging talk and texts on sustained topics and in different genres of oral and written language (see pp. 106–8).

So a certain sort of early "language ability" is what causes both phonemic awareness and learning to read early and well. True enough, but we must be careful here or the term "language ability" can lead us into massive amounts of confusion. It is a very poor term indeed. I turn to this issue now.

Language ability

Do poor children have less "language ability" than rich ones? The way the term is being used above certainly makes it sound as if they do. But no, they don't. Linguists have known for years that all children – including poor children – have impressive language ability. The vast majority of children enter school with vocabularies fully fit for everyday life, with complex grammar and with deep understandings of experiences and stories. It has been decades since anyone believed that poor and minority children entered school with "no language" (Labov, 1972; Gee, 1996). Every human being, barring those with very serious disorders, acquires a complex native language early in life – a language fully fit for the task of leading daily life in a human culture.

When Snow *et al.* (1998) uses the term "language ability," it is not really talking about language ability in the sense in which all human beings acquire a fully fit native language. We have already pointed out earlier that it never happens (barring those with quite serious disorders) that Janie gets relative clauses and Johnnie doesn't when they are both young children acquiring English as their native language. Rather, the report is talking about specific early "ways with words" that prepare children to do well when they enter school. We can't really understand what these are unless we understand some very basic and important things about language itself.

People think of a language like English as one thing – "a language." Actually, it's not one thing, it's many things. There are many different varieties of English. Some of these are different dialects spoken in different regions of the country or by different sociocultural groups. Some of them are different varieties of language used by different occupations or for different specific purposes: for example, the language of bookies, lawyers, or video game players.

I want to introduce an important distinction between two different types of varieties of language. This is the distinction between vernacular varieties and specialist varieties. Every human being, early in life, acquires a vernacular variety of his or her native language. This form is used for face-to-face conversation and for "everyday" purposes. Different groups of people speak different dialects of the vernacular, connected to their family and community. Thus a person's vernacular dialect is closely connected to his or her initial sense of self and belonging in life.

After the acquisition of their vernacular variety has started, people often also go on to acquire various non-vernacular specialist varieties of language used for special purposes and activities. For example, they may acquire a way of talking (and writing) about fundamentalist Christian theology, video games, or bird-watching. Specialist varieties of language are different – sometimes in small ways, sometimes in large ways – from people's vernacular varieties of language.

One category of specialist varieties of language is what we can call academic varieties of language: that is, the varieties of language connected to learning and using information from academic or school-based content areas (Gee 2002; Schleppegrell 2004; Schleppegrell and Cecilia Colombi 2002) The varieties of language used in (different branches) of biology, physics, law, or literary criticism fall into this category. Many people can't stand these varieties of language (as I well know when non-academics review my books and castigate them for their "jargon," despite the fact that I try to keep it at a minimum).

Some texts are, of course, written in vernacular varieties of language: for example, some letters, email, and children's books. But the vast majority of texts in the modern world are not written in the vernacular, but in some specialist variety of language. People who learn to read the vernacular often have great trouble reading texts written in specialist varieties of language. Of course there are some texts written in specialist varieties of language (e.g. nuclear physics) that many very good readers can't read.

Specialist varieties of language, whether academic or not, often have both spoken forms and written ones, and these may themselves differ from each other. For example, a physicist or computer scientist can write in the language of physics or computer science and he or she can talk a version of it too (e.g. in a lecture).

Figure 1 lists the distinctions I am making here.

It is obvious that once we talk about learning to read and speak specialist varieties of language, it is hard to separate learning to read and speak this way

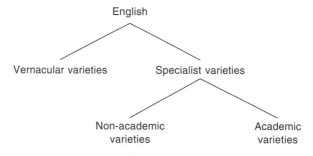

Figure 1 Varieties of language.

from learning the sorts of content or information that the specialist language is typically used to convey. That content is accessible through the specialist variety of language and, in turn, that content is what gives meaning to that form of language. The two – content and language – are married.

Of course one key area where specialist varieties of language differ from vernacular ones is in vocabulary. But they also often differ in syntax and discourse features as well ("syntax" means the internal structure of sentences; "discourse" here means how sentences are related to each other across a text and what sorts of things can or cannot be said in a particular type of text). For example, suppose someone is studying the development of hornworms (cute green caterpillars with yellow horns). Contrast the vernacular sentence "Hornworms sure vary a lot in how well they grow" to the (academic) specialist sentence "Hornworm growth exhibits a significant amount of variation."

The specialist version differs in vocabulary (e.g. "exhibits"). But it also differs in syntactic structure as well. Verbs naming dynamic processes in the vernacular version (e.g. "vary", "grow") show up as nouns naming abstract things in the specialist version ("variation", "growth"). The vernacular sentence makes the hornworms (cute little caterpillars) the subject/topic of the sentence, but the specialist sentence makes hornworm growth (a measurable trait for hornworms) the subject/topic. A verb–adverb pair in the vernacular version ("vary a lot") turns into a verb plus a complex noun phrase in the specialist version ("exhibits a significant amount of variation").

Though we do not have space to pursue the matter fully here, specialist varieties of language also differ from vernacular varieties at the discourse level. We can see this even with our two sentences. Note that the specialist version does not allow an emotional word like "sure" that occurs in the vernacular version. We would not usually write or say "Hornworm growth sure exhibits a significant amount of variation." There is nothing wrong with this sentence syntactically. It's just that we don't normally speak or write this way in this variety of language. It doesn't "go with" the other things we say or write in this variety. At the cross-sentential level, specialist languages use many devices to connect, contrast, and integrate sentences across stretches of text that are not used as frequently, nor in exactly in the same way, in vernacular varieties of language (like my phrase "at the cross-sentential level" at the beginning of this sentence).

Specialist languages, of course, draw on many of the grammatical resources that exist also in vernacular varieties of language. For example, any vernacular variety of English can make a noun (like "growth") out of a verb (like "grow"). But to know the specialist language you have to know that this is done regularly in such a variety, you have to know why (what its function is in the specialist language), and you have to know how and why doing this goes together with doing a host of other related things (for example, using a subject like "hornworm growth," rather than "hornworms," or avoiding emotive words like "sure"). Any variety of a language uses certain patterns of resources, and to know the language you have to be able to recognize and use these patterns. This is much like recognizing that the pattern of clothing "sun hat, swim suit, and thongs" means someone is going to the beach.

So what, for heaven's sake, has all this got to do with poor kids having a hard time learning to read in school? School is, as it is presently constituted, ultimately all about learning specialist varieties of language, in particular academic varieties of language connected to content areas. Some children bring early prototypes of academic varieties of language to school – prototypes they have learned at home. Some do not. Those who do bring prototypes of academic language to school have what Snow *et al.* (1998) refer to as "early language ability." Those who don't don't, despite the fact that they have perfectly good vernacular varieties of language and, as we will see below, a plethora of language abilities that don't get rewarded at school.

In the next chapter I will demonstrate exactly what I mean by "early prototypes of academic varieties of language." The examples will be familiar to many. They are things like children doing pretend readings of books, that sound like the child is reading a real book, or children reporting at dinnertime on their day in a fashion that sounds like a school report. Some families encourage their children to do these things, while others don't – some, in fact, wouldn't be caught dead doing some of these things.

For simplicity's sake, I will now sometimes use the term "academic language" (as I just did in the last paragraph) as a shorthand form for "academic varieties of language." I ask the reader to keep in mind that "academic language" is not one thing, but a set of different, though related, varieties.

The failure to bring prototypes of academic language to school is exactly why the fourth-grade slump happens. Children who do not bring such prototypes to school can learn to read in the sense of decoding vernacular language that is written down. But they cannot later read the early versions of academic varieties of language they see in books and sometimes hear teachers speak around fourth grade (often earlier today). This is because schools do not start the academic language acquisition process for these children – a process that has already started at home for other children. Rather, they teach these children to "read" only in the sense of being able to do phonics and dealing with the superficial literal meanings of words mostly in the vernacular. Poor children suffer the same sort of plight that someone who tries to pass French 4 without French 1, French 2, and French 3 does. This problem doesn't say much about the children's abilities, though it says a lot about the schooling system they are in.

On the other hand, schools allow children who bring early prototypes of academic languages with them to school to practice and acquire more complicated varieties of academic language step by step. They bring French 1 – sometimes French 2 – with them to school and can make the leap to French 4 in fourth grade, thanks to their ongoing acceleration at home, even if they have not had much focus on academic varieties of language in the early grades. Of course they are often in affluent schools, and in fact get lots of practice with academic varieties of language at school starting in the early grades. By fourth grade they are doing middle-school work.

So we need to move on to see what it means to learn early prototypes of academic language at home. We will see that ability per se does not have much to do with the matter. I turn to this topic in the next chapter.

3

LANGUAGE AND IDENTITY
AT HOME

Early prototypes of academic language

Specialist language varieties, whether the language of video gamers or of physicists, are technologies, just like computers, televisions, or phones. Technologies are tools that allow us to do certain things. Despite many claims to the contrary, technologies have no effects – good or bad – apart from the specific situations or settings in which they are used. In different situations they have different effects. When children watch television with an adult who gets them to think and talk about what they are watching, it can be good for the children's cognitive growth. When they watch alone and passively, it can be bad (Greenfield 1984). It's the situation that counts.

The situations about which we are concerned when we look at early literacy development in the home are "social practices": that is, the ways in which oral and written language are used when people do things together. What we are concerned with here are early practices involving language that are good for at least one thing: namely, doing well in school. Whether they are good for anything else is a topic we will take up later.

In order to make clear what I mean by early prototypes of academic language, set within home-based social practices, I will offer several different examples. Consider first, then, the following story told by a five-year-old Anglo-American middle-class girl whom we will call "Jennie" (Gee 1996). Jennie was holding a book and pretending to read it to her mother and older sister:

Jennie's story

This is a story about some kids who were once friends,
But got into a big fight, and were not.

You can read along in your story book.
I'm gonna read aloud.

How the Friends Got Unfriend

Once upon a time there was three boys 'n three girls.
They were named Betty Lou, Pallis, and Parshin, were the girls,

21

And Michael, Jason, and Aaron were the boys.
They were friends.

The boys would play Transformers,
And the girls would play Cabbage Patches.

But then one day they got into a fight on who would be which team.
It was a very bad fight.
They were punching,
And they were pulling,
And they were banging.

Then all of a sudden the sky turned dark,
The rain began to fall,
There was lightning going on,
And they were not friends.

Then um the mothers came shooting out 'n saying,
"What are you punching for?
You are going to be punished for a whole year".

The end.

Wasn't it fun reading together?
Let's do it again, real soon!

Jennie is pretending to read a book (holding a book in front of her), while she tells a story in a "literary" way: a story about a real fight that had occurred at her birthday party. Jennie's pretend reading took place as part of her primary socialization as a member of her family at home. One of the common social practices in this home was for Jennie's mother to read a book to her two daughters. Sometimes the older daughter, who could read, would take a turn reading a book. In this case, Jennie asked for a turn, despite the fact that she could not read, and told the story above, while holding a book and pretending to be reading from it.

Jennie turned a real everyday event – one which we know she had already told in her everyday vernacular language to other adults – into a "literary" story. Let's consider the ways in which Jennie's text can be construed as "literary" in a school-based way. First, she announces the beginning and end of her story and offers an initial summary or overview of what the story will be about: "This is a story about some kids who were once friends, but got into a big fight and were not . . . The end."

Second, she adopts a frame that mimics story book reading as it is often done by teachers and other teacherly adults: "You can read along in your story book. I'm gonna read aloud . . . Wasn't it fun reading together? Let's do it again, real soon." This is all said in a tone of voice quite different from when she is "reading" the story proper. Her tone of voice sounds as if she is imitating an adult.

Third, she offers a title for her story: "How the friends got unfriend." In everyday oral story-telling, we do not normally offer a title.

Fourth, she uses syntactic structures that are typical of literary books, not everyday vernacular talk: "Once upon a time there was three boys 'n three girls. They were named Betty Lou, Pallis, and Parshin, were the girls. And Michael, Jason, and Aaron were the boys. They were friends." In everyday story-telling we don't say "Once upon a time." In everyday speech, we don't say things like "And Michael, Jason, and Aaron were the boys," but rather "The boys were Michael, Jason, and Aaron."

Fifth, she uses lots of literary sorts of repetition and parallelism: "The boys would play Transformers. And the girls would play Cabbage Patches. But then one day they got into a fight on who would be which team. It was a very bad fight. They were punching. And they were pulling. And they were banging." Here Jennie sets up the parallelism "the boys . . . the girls," "play Transformers . . . play Cabbage Patches," and then creates stylistic repetition with "punching . . . pulling . . . banging."

Sixth, Jennie uses a specific (and very old) figurative device that is common in "high literature," namely, the "sympathetic fallacy" (Abrams 1953). This is a literary device in which nature, or the cosmos, is treated as if it is "in step with" human affairs (e.g. the beauty and peace of a sunset matches the inner peace of the elderly poet resigned to the approach of the end of life). The device is common in the Bible, in poetry, in some sorts of novels, and even in film. In Jennie's story the sympathetic fallacy is a central organizing device. The fight between the girls and boys is immediately followed by the sky turning dark and lightning flashing. Then we get the line: "and they were not friends" and the mothers come on the scene to punish the children for their transgression. Between the "evil" event and its "bad" effect, nature has its say. Human happenings here are "unnatural" – out of step with the nature of things – and nature shows its disapproval by the sky turning dark and filling with lightning.

The sympathetic fallacy functions in Jennie's story in much the same way as it does in "high literature." The story suggests that gender differences (boy versus girl) are associated with different interests (Transformers versus Cabbage Patches) and that these different interests inevitably lead to conflict when male and female try to be "equal" or sort themselves on other grounds than gender ("a fight on who would be which team": the actual fight at her party had been about mixing genders on the teams). The children are punished for transgressing gender lines, but only after the use of the sympathetic fallacy has suggested that division by gender, and the conflicts which transgressing this division leads to, are sanctioned by nature, are "natural" and "inevitable," not merely conventional or constructed in the very act of play itself.

What is happening here is that a little girl, who cannot yet "really" read, is learning and practicing non-vernacular forms of language associated with school and schooling. She is doing this as part of her initial primary identity in life as "a person like us": that is, as a member of a particular family belonging to a particular social group. "People like us" do and value "things like this," which involve special sorts of language – sorts that just happen to be used widely in school and in books found at school.

Of course Jennie is no master of this sort of language. She is in the initial stages of a long language acquisition process in which she will eventually learn to speak and write a number of different specialist varieties of language connected to schooling and academic domains. These specialist varieties of language are themselves connected to certain sorts of identities (e.g. "literary writer," "scientist"). What is happening is that Jennie is learning to identify certain sorts of school-related identities with her primary home-based identity by forming an association between these two identities. This association, taking place at home as part of her early socialization, is deeply emotionally laden. It is stored deeply in her brain and personality.

Let's consider another example. This example involves a first-grade boy we will call Brian. Brian learned to read in first grade, thanks in part, as we will see below, to Pokémon. At home, Brian had lots of books, a good many of which were not story books, but informational texts. One day, coming home from an outing, when asked what he wanted to do, he announced to his mother that he wanted to write a "report." He could not yet write at all well, so he asked to dictate the report to his mother. Here is what he dictated:

Brian's report

EARTH
Earth moves so everything else moves with it.

PLUTO
Pluto is the most farthest planet from the sun. Also the most coolest.

Some planets are dangerous. Some have carbon monoxide and some have asteroids. Some planets that are near the sun are hot; others that are a little farther away are warm. The sun is the hottest source of heat in the whole wide world.

Brian

Brian's text shows an emerging understanding of how expository informational language is organized. The text has three sections, one on Earth, one on Pluto, and one on planets more generally. Each section is itself organized in terms of causality: everything else moves *because* the Earth moves (note the "so"); Pluto is coolest *because* it is farthest from the Sun; some planets are dangerous *because* they have carbon monoxide or asteroids; some planets are hot *because* they are near the Sun, others are warm *because* they are a little further away. The text ends on a summary statement about the Sun, an entity which is centrally involved with many of the claims in the text.

The text is mostly in the vernacular, but there are initial attempts at non-vernacular language. First, vernacular language tends to have many subjects which are pronouns (e.g. "she said this", "he did that"), while this text has sentences all of whose subjects are nouns or noun phrases (e.g. "Pluto" or "some planets"). Second, a phrase like "the hottest source of heat in the whole wide world" mixes vernacular (e.g. "whole wide world") and specialist (e.g. "source of heat") language.

While children are often immersed in stories at home and early on in school, informational texts and texts composed of casual ("because") reasoning play a bigger and bigger role as the child goes on in school. It is just such texts that children who experience the fourth-grade slump have trouble reading, for example in their textbooks. But here is a child who is engaging in such language as part of his play time at home. He is doing this with his mother, for fun. Once again, this child is being socialized in such a way that a school-based language practice is utterly melded with how he is becoming a "person like us": that is, a member of his family. He clearly will not see academic varieties of language as "foreign" to his sense of self as he goes through school.

Of course Brian is not yet very adept at expository language. He is at the beginning of his apprenticeship. But that is the point. He is at the beginning of an apprenticeship that some children don't seriously start until the later grades, when the academic-like demands made on their reading, writing, and listening skills swamp them. Ironically, for Brian, like many other children, first grade was largely about stories and simple texts that were easy to decode. He experienced much more complicated informational texts and practices at home. While the text above was collected early in his first-grade experience, by the end of the first grade, he read at the fifth-grade level. He ended up reading on the Internet, in books, and in his video games much more complicated and much more academic-like language than he read in his first-grade school texts.

I want now to turn to a last example: an example that looks rather different. This example involves Brian as well. Brian had not been able to read when he entered kindergarten. He had, however, gotten a Nintendo Game Boy, a hand-held video game player. He had already developed a passion for Pokémon and wanted to play the Pokémon games. These games involve lots of reading of dialogue and informational statements about the Pokémon's names, types, attacks, and other attributes, as well as about the game world and the human characters in that world. Brain could not read. So his mother played the game with him, at first reading everything for him and learning to play the game (which is complicated) with him step by step. It was this experience, coupled with much interaction with the Pokémon universe (via cards, figures, books, and the Internet), that both motivated him to want to read and taught him how to read, along with a good first-grade teacher. But the first-grade teacher, for Brian and other kids like him, was the cherry on top of ice cream that had already been served.

Brian used Pokémon to practice reading at home much more than he practiced any sort of reading at school. Furthermore, the Pokémon texts were much more complicated than what he saw in school. For instance, here, at random, are some of the sorts of things Brian would read when he read Pokémon cards or searched the Internet for information on Pokémon (http://www.pokemon-cards-and-pokemon-pictures.com/evolving.html):

> Description: Kadabra relies on a strong mind rather than a powerful body to win. It can send out waves of mental energy that cause headaches at close range.

> Description: Experts believe that Alakazam's brain is as powerful as any supercomputer. Its incredible psychic abilities back up that belief.

Brian's reading connected to Pokémon was fully embedded in his interactions with both parents – interactions that were not defined as learning, but as playing and being socialized into his family. Here, once again, specialist language – and much of this language is not unlike the forms of language some academic domains use – is caught up in all the social and emotional valences of the child's early socialization in life as a member of a family of a certain type.

But we can go further here. Let's look at Brian's interaction with the video game *Pikmin*, a game he played in first grade (Gee 2003). *Pikmin* is a game for the Nintendo Game Cube, rated "E," a game acceptable for all ages. In *Pikmin*, the player takes on the role of Captain Olimar, a small (he's about the size of an American quarter), bald, big-eared, bulbous-nosed spaceman who crashes into an unfamiliar planet when a comet hits his spaceship. Captain Olimar (i.e. the player) must collect the spaceship's lost parts, scattered throughout the planet, while relying on his spacesuit to protect him from the planet's poisonous atmosphere. To make matters more complicated, the spacesuit's life support will fail after 30 days, so the captain (the player) must find all the missing parts in 30 days (each day is 15 minutes of game-time play).

However, Captain Olimar gets help. Soon after arriving on the strange planet, he comes upon native life that is willing to aid him. Sprouts dispensed from a large onion-like creature yield tiny (they're even smaller than Captain Olimar) cute creatures that Olimar names "Pikmin" after a carrot from his home planet. These little creatures appear to be quite taken with Olimar and follow his directions without question. Captain Olimar learns to raise Pikmin of three different colors (red, yellow, and blue), each of which has different skills. He learns, as well, to train them so that each Pikmin, regardless of color, can grow through three different ever stronger forms: Pikmin sprouting a leaf, a bud, or a flower from their heads.

His colorful Pikmin following him as his army, Captain Olimar uses them to attack dangerous creatures, tear down stone walls, build bridges, and explore a great many areas of the strange planet in search of the missing parts to his spaceship. While Captain Olimar can replace killed Pikmin from remaining Pikmin, he must, however, ensure that at no point do all his Pikmin perish – an event called, by the game and by Brian, "an extinction event."

When Brian had recovered 5 of the spaceship's 30 missing parts, he was able to search in a new area called the Forest's Navel. This area had a much harsher and more dangerous-looking landscape than the previous areas the child had been in. It had different dangerous creatures, including a number of closely grouped ones that breathed fire. And the background music had changed considerably. Since the player has already found five parts, the game assumes that he or she is now more adept than when he began the game; thus the landscape and creatures get harder to deal with, offering a bigger challenge. At the same time, these changes in features communicate a new mood, changing the tone of the game from a cute fairy tale to a somewhat darker struggle for survival.

Brian was able to think about and comment on these changes to his father, who often sat with him while he played the game. He said that the music was now "scary" and the landscape much harsher-looking than the ones he had previously been in. He said that this meant things were going to get harder. Furthermore, he was aware that the changes signaled that he needed to rethink some of his strategies, as well his relationship to the game. He was even able to comment on the fact that the earlier parts of the game had made it appear more appropriate for a child his age than did the Forest Navel area and considered whether the game was now "too scary" or not. He said he would, at least initially, use a strategy of exploring the new area only a little bit, avoiding the fire-breathing creatures, and then return to old areas with new resources (e.g. blue Pikmin) he found in the Forest Navel area so he could get more parts in these old areas more quickly and easily.

What we are dealing with here is talking and thinking about the (internal) design of the game – about the game as a complex system of interrelated parts meant to engage and even manipulate the player in certain ways. This is metalevel thinking: thinking about the game as a system and a designed space, and not just playing within the game moment by moment. Brian's father had repeatedly encouraged this sort of talking and thinking about the design of the game. Schooling and academic domains regularly demand that learners don't just do things, but think about what they are doing and why. They regularly demand, too, that learners think about content (e.g. physics, literature, or social studies) not just as facts, but as a complex system (a complex set of relationships) with a certain sort of design. Such thinking requires forms of language suited for talking about thinking itself and for talking about complex relationships.

Now, to conclude this section, there are two important things to say about our three examples. First, none of them are important in and of themselves. They are simply examples of what happens in some children's homes thousands of times. These children get lots of early practice with forms of language (connected to forms of thinking) that pay off in school and pay off more and more as the child moves towards the later grades.

This practice starts very early: for example, when a parent asks a small child at dinner to report on what has happened at home during the day or on a trip to the park and helps the child to give the report in explicit language that is more like a book than normal everyday language between intimates. It happens even earlier in conversations like the one below between a 29-month-old child and his parents (from Snow, 1986: p. 82):

Child: Pancakes away.
         Duh duh stomach.
Mother: Pancakes away in the stomach, yes, that's right.
Child: Eat apples.
Mother: Eating apples on our pancakes, aren't we?
Child: On our pancakes.
Mother: You like apples on your pancakes?
Child: Eating apples.
         Hard.
Mother: What?
         Hard to do the apples, isn't it?
Child: More pancakes.
Father: You want more pancakes?
Child: Those are daddy's.
Father: Daddy's gonna have his pancakes now.
Child: Ne ne one a daddy's.
         Ne ne one in the plate.
         Right there.
Father: You want some more on your plate?

This conversation is a sort of interactive slot-and-filler activity centered around adding more and more descriptive and lexically explicit detail around a single topic. One of the core features of school-based and academic varieties of language is that they demand that learners learn how to produce lots of explicit language around one focused topic. This later becomes a particular hallmark of writing things like essays.

Second, these language practices are done in these homes not just or primarily to give children certain skills, but rather to give them certain values, attitudes, motivations, ways of interacting, and perspectives, all of which are more important than mere skills for success later in school. These homes meld the primary identity or sense of self that each child picks up through his or her early socialization within a family with ways with words associated with specialist academic identities the child will see more and more as he or she moves through school and society.

Good language that doesn't pay off in school

I said before that poor children do not have less language ability than rich ones. Indeed, many poor families also engage their children in complex language practices at home. The problem is that these practices often do not pay off in school, though of course we could imagine school changing in such a way that they did. And indeed they should.

Let me give one example of a language practice found commonly among African-American children (though of course not all African-American children – they need to have had lots of contact with some important aspects of a specific variety of African-American culture). I print below a story that was told at sharing time in school by an African-American first-grade girl we will call "Leona" (Gee 1996). Leona came from a lower socioeconomic home. The type of story-telling Leona engages in has now been well documented among African-Americans, though of course here we will see a seven-year-old version of it. Leona has learned to tell stories this way at home and in her community.

I will point out below that Leona's stories at sharing time were not well received by her teacher, who often told her to sit down because she was "rambling on." I have printed Leona's story in terms of lines and stanzas to help bring out its poetic qualities. The form "an'" below is a normal usage in many varieties of vernacular English and here has the function of marking the beginnings of lines; forms like "bakin'" are also typical of many varieties of English vernacular. There is nothing "wrong" about these forms. Chances are that the readers of this book, whether they are aware of it or not, regularly use both of these forms in their vernacular English, though they may well not use "an'" in the function of a poetic line beginner:

Leona's story

FRAME
STANZA 1
1. Today
2. it's Friday the 13th
3. an' it's bad luck day
4. an' my grandmother's birthday is on bad luck day

EPISODE 1: MAKING CAKES (5–14)
STANZA 2
5. an' my mother's bakin' a cake
6. an' I went up my grandmother's house while my mother's bakin' a cake
7. an' my mother was bakin' a cheese cake
8. my grandmother was bakin' a whipped cream cup cakes

STANZA 3
9. an' we both went over my mother's house
10. an' then my grandmother had made a chocolate cake
11. an' then we went over my aunt's house
12. an' she had make a cake

STANZA 4

13. an' everybody had made a cake for nana
14. so we came out with six cakes

EPISODE 2: GRANDMOTHER EATS CAKES (15–34)
STANZA 5

15. last night
16. my grandmother snuck out
17. an' she ate all the cake
18. an' we hadda make more

STANZA 6

19. an' we was sleepin'
20. an' she went in the room
21. an' gobbled em up
22. an' we hadda bake a whole bunch more

STANZA 7

23. she said mmmm
24. she had all chocolate on her face, cream, strawberries
25. she said mmmm
26. that was good

STANZA 8

27. an' then an' then all came out
28. an' my grandmother had ate all of it
29. she said "what's this cheese cake doin' here" – she didn't like cheese cakes
30. an' she told everybody that she didn't like cheese cakes

STANZA 9

31. an' we kept makin' cakes
32. an' she kept eatin' 'em
33. an' we finally got tired of makin' cakes
34. an' so we all ate 'em

EPISODE 3: GRANDMOTHER GOES OUTSIDE THE HOME (35–47)
NON-NARRATIVE SECTION (35–41)
STANZA 10

35. an' now
36. today's my grandmother's birthday
37. an' a lot o'people's makin' a cake again
38. but my grandmother is goin' t'get her own cake at her bakery
39. an' she's gonna come out with a cake
40. that we didn't make
41. cause she likes chocolate cream

ENDING
STANZA 11
42. an' I went t'the bakery with her
43. an' my grandmother ate cup cakes
44. an' an' she finally got sick on today
45. an' she was growling like a dog cause she ate so many cakes

FRAME
STANZA 12
46. an' I finally told her that it was
47. it was Friday the thirteenth bad luck day

Leona groups her lines into stanzas wherein each line tends to have a parallel structure with other lines in the stanza and to match them in content, just as biblical poetry (e.g. in the Psalms), the narratives of many oral cultures (e.g. Homer), and much "free verse" (e.g. the poetry of Walt Whitman) do. Furthermore, the lines in a stanza sound as if they go together, by tending to be said at the same rate and with little hesitation between the lines. Leona's stanzas are very often four lines long, though they are sometimes two lines long. Thus Leona's stanzas show intricate structure and patterning, taking on some of the properties of stanzas in poetry.

Look, for example, at Stanza 2:

an' my mother's bakin' a cake
an' I went up my grandmother's house while my mother's bakin' a cake
an' my mother was bakin' a cheese cake
my grandmother was bakin' a whipped cream cup cakes

This stanza is full of complex parallelism and repetition. Notice that every line ends on "cake." The first and second lines repeat "bakin' a cake," while the third and fourth repeat "bakin' a [kind of] cake." The first and third lines repeat "my mother," while the second and fourth repeat "my grandmother." Thus these lines are fully saturated with pattern and are tightly knit together.

That this sort of parallelism is really part of Leona's speech production process is shown by the speech error in the fourth line. The line-end pattern that Leona is using in this stanza is essentially: . . . bakin' a cake / . . . bakin' a cake / . . . bakin' a TYPE of cake / . . . bakin' a TYPE of cake (an aabb "rhyme" scheme). However, her fourth line ends on a plural noun ("cup cakes"), and so cannot take the singular article "a" required by the formal pattern. Nonetheless, driven by the pattern, Leona says in the fourth line "bakin' a whipped cream cup cakes." It is as if she is operating with slots that are to be filled in ways partially determined by what has come before (this type of composing process is common in "oral poetry" in many cultures).

Or, to take another example, Stanza 3:

an' we both went over my mother's house
an' then my grandmother had made a chocolate cake
an' then we went over my aunt's house
an' she had made a cake

This stanza has a clear abab structure: lines 1 and 3 repeat "we . . . went over my X's house," while lines 2 and 4 repeat that someone "had made a cake." Notice, too, the lines end "house . . . cake . . . house . . . cake" (abab).

There are levels of organization in Leona's story beyond lines and stanzas. If we look at the content of Leona's narrative as a whole, it clearly falls into larger units that we can call "episodes." In the text above, I have labeled each of the episodes. The breakdown into episodes in terms of topics or themes is fairly straightforward and obvious. In turn, it is confirmed by other structural properties of the texts. The first episode is about baking cakes, the second about the grandmother eating the cakes, and the third is about getting a cake at a bakery. The second episode begins on a temporal adverb ("last night"); the third does also ("an' now"). The first episode, of course, is understood to be in the scope of the opening temporal adverb in the opening frame ("today").

Let's now look a moment at what I have labeled the "non-narrative" section of Leona's story (lines 35–41). This is a place where she momentarily breaks out of the story's mainline events:

an' now
today's my grandmother's birthday
an' a lot o'people's makin' a cake again
but my grandmother is goin' t'get her own cake at her bakery
an' she's gonna come out with a cake
that we didn't make
cause she likes chocolate cream

This portion of Leona's story involves generic summary statements, not the discrete events that a story is made out of. Thus we get a brief break in the narrative here. There are two things to note about the language of this portion. First, it is more complicated syntactically than the other parts of the text. Second, it does not by any means fit as nicely the line and stanza structures we have been using.

This portion of Leona's story serves as what the sociolinguist William Labov (1972; Labov and Waletsky 1967) has called "evaluation'" (which, he points out, often occurs before the ending in the narratives of African-American teenagers), giving an indication of the point of the story and what Leona considers makes it "tellable." Further, these lines serve as transitions between the body of the story and the ending, giving Leona space and time to plan the ending. They thus serve as aids both to the listener and to the speaker. This part of the story is crucial to its interpretation (see below).

We have not, thus far, gotten at the deeper meanings of Leona's story, just its structure. Given the amount of parallelism and repetition in her text, clearly Leona is not primarily interested in making rapid and linear progress to "the point." Rather, she is interested in creating a pattern out of language, within and across her stanzas: a pattern which will generate meaning through the sets of relationships and contrasts which it sets up, like the multiple relationships and contrasts – the points of contact and stress – in a painting or a poem (Frank 1963).

And what might that meaning be? Of course there are always multiple plausible interpretations of a text (and many non-plausible ones as well). But if we follow the clues or guides Leona has placed in the organization of her text, and are sensitive to her culture, we can offer a "reading" that accepts the invitations of her language.

The non-narrative "evaluative" section in stanza 10 (lines 35–41) suggests that there is something significant in the fact that the grandmother is going to get a cake at the bakery and thus "come out with a cake that we [the family] didn't make." And indeed the story as a whole places a great deal of emphasis on the production of cakes within the family, a production that doesn't cease even when the grandmother keeps eating them.

The grandmother, the matriarch and repository of the culture's norms, is behaving like a child, sneaking out and eating the cakes and rudely announcing that she doesn't like "cheese cake," even though the cake has been made by her relatives for her birthday. It must intrigue the child narrator that the grandmother can behave this way and no one gets angry with her; in fact the family simply makes more cakes. Surely the story carries some messages about family loyalty and respect for age. But it also, I would argue, raises a problem: the matriarch, the guardian of culturally normative behavior, is behaving in such a way as to violate the home and culture's canons of polite behavior. What might the sanctions be for such a violation? And what is the deeper meaning of the grandmother's violation? Like all real stories, this one raises real problems – problems that the story attempts to resolve in a satisfying manner.

We can get to this deeper level of the text if we consider the constant use of and play on the word "cake" in the story. The story, in fact, contains a humorous paradox about cakes: the grandmother eats innumerable (normal-sized) cakes at home, made by her relatives, and never gets sick. Then she goes outside the home, buys little cakes ("cup cakes") at the bakery, and not only does she get sick, she "growls like a dog": that is, she loses her human status and turns into an animal. Why?

What I would argue is this: the grandmother is learning, and the child narrator is enacting, a lesson about signs or symbols. A birthday cake is a material object, but it is also an immaterial sign or symbol of kinship, when made within the family – a celebration of birth and family membership. The cake at the bakery looks the same, but it is a duplicitous symbol – it is not actually a sign of kinship; rather it is a commodity that non-kin have made to sell, not to celebrate the birth of someone they care about. To mistake the baker's cake for a true symbol of birth and kin is to think, mistakenly, that signs have meaning outside the contexts that give them meaning.

In the context of the family, the cake means kinship and celebration; in the context of the bakery and market society it signals exchange and commodities. The grandmother, in her greed, overvalues the material base of the sign (its cakehood) and misses its meaning, undervaluing the network of kin that gives meaning to the cakes. This is particularly dangerous when we consider that the grandmother is a senior representative of the family and the culture. Her penalty is to momentarily lose her human status – that is, the status of a giver and taker of symbolic meaning. She becomes an animal, merely an eater.

And now, of course, I must face the inevitable question: could this seven-year-old really have meant this? Could she really have this sophisticated a theory of signs? I would argue that these questions seem so compelling to us because we think meaning is a matter of privatized intentions locked in people's heads and indicative of their individual "intelligence" or "skill." But once we deny this view of meaning, the questions lose most of their force; in fact, they become somewhat odd.

Leona has inherited, by her apprenticeship in the social practices of her community, ways of making sense of experience that, in fact, have a long and rich history going back thousands of years. This enculturation/apprenticeship has given her certain forms of language, ranging from devices at the word and clause level, through the stanza level, to the story level as a whole – forms of language which are intimately connected to forms of life (Wittgenstein 1958). These forms of language are not merely structural; rather they encapsulate and carry through time and space meanings shared by and lived out in a variety of ways by the social group. As for the specific theme of the cakes story, we can point out that African-Americans, as an oppressed group, have long cared deeply about reading signs correctly so as to protect themselves and their children.

So Leona has, like the more financially well-off white children we looked at earlier, picked up some very sophisticated language practices at home. However, they did not pay off for her at school. Why? The teacher heard her as rambling. In fact, the teacher often thought Leona was going to start off on another story when she got to what we have called her "evaluative" section (lines 35–41 above) – ironically a section marking the coming end of her story. It was here she normally got told to sit down, just as she was about to finish.

Research has shown that teachers at sharing time are often not listening for stories like Leona's. Rather they expect blow-by-blow narratives or reports. Reports about how to make candles step by step or an event-by-event narrative about going swimming with one's mother were acceptable and well received by Leona's teacher. These sorts of sharing-time turns are, in fact, prototypes of academic language of the sort we examined in the last section. They stress linear step-by-step events or facts organized around one topic expressed with no poetry or emotion: certainly a form of language found often in school subjects and academic domains alike. Leona's story does not, to teachers, sound like an early prototype of school-based or academic language, though a recipe on how to make a candle does.

Jennie's story above is itself too poetic to be used at a sharing time session in most schools, and she would not have told her story in such a situation. On the other hand, her story sounds more like a book than does Leona's. Thus such a story would get accepted elsewhere in the curriculum as an early prototype of school-based language, especially literary language, while Leona's wouldn't.

Could Leona's story-telling language practice have been fruitfully recruited by the school? Of course. Her sort of oral poetry has historically been the very foundation and origin of literature – think of Homer, think of Chaucer. She brought an opening for success with her to school, just as the richer kids had. However, they were encouraged to walk through their gates. Leona's gate was closed in her face. She was only a first-grader.

However, to praise Leona's talent and demand that schools recognize and use it should not blind us from worrying about the fact that she does not bring prototypes of academic language to school. As long as schools are organized as they are – and they have historically been impervious to change – she will suffer for that. The school will start her apprenticeship on academic language too late – right when she is ready to be a victim of the fourth-grade slump.

Reading and identity

I want to end this chapter by discussing one of the ways in which learning, identity, and poverty or oppression are interconnected. Earlier we had been pursuing the traditionalists' claim that poor readers failed to learn to read well because they received poor skills training. We saw that there were good reasons to reject this claim. Now we will see another one.

As we have pointed out, in the United States poor readers are concentrated "in certain ethnic groups and in poor, urban neighborhoods and rural towns," as the report *Preventing reading difficulties in young children* (Snow *et al.* 1998) put it (p. 98). Consider the quote below from this report:

> average reading achievement has not changed markedly over the last 20 years (NAEP 1997). And following a gain by black children from 1970 to 1980, the white-black gap has remained roughly constant for the last 16 years . . .

> Americans do very well in international comparisons of reading – much better, comparatively speaking, than they do on math or science. In a 1992 study comparing reading skill levels among 9-year-olds in 18 Western nations, U.S. students scored among the highest levels and were second only to students in Finland . . . (Elley 1992).

(pp. 97–8)

Here the report mentions the now well-known and much studied issue that from the late 1960s to the early 1980s, the Black–White gap in IQ test scores and other sorts of test scores, including reading tests, was fast closing (Neisser 1998; Jencks and Phillips 1998). This heartening progress ceased in the 1980s. Clearly, these factors were, whatever else they were, powerful "reading interventions," since they significantly increased the reading scores of "at risk" children.

Though the matter is controversial (Neisser 1998; Jencks and Phillips 1998), these factors may have been closely connected to the sorts of social programs (stemming originally from Johnson's "War on Poverty") that were dismantled in the 1980s and 90s (Grissmer *et al.* 1998: pp. 221–3). However that may be, the test scores were going up at a time that integration was also increasing. By the mid-1980s integration increases ceased and the society became more segregated instead, a trend that continues today. Ironically, the progress made on reading tests during the time the Black–White gap was closing was far greater, in quantitative terms (Hedges and Nowell 1998), than the results of any of the interventions (e.g. early phonemic awareness training) that Snow *et al.* (1998) discuss and advocate.

The following remarks from Snow *et al.* (1998) are typical of the sense of paradox bordering on outright contradiction that pervades this report and much traditionalist work on the issue of poor and minority children:

> for students in schools in which more than 75 percent of all students received free or reduced-price lunches (a measure of high poverty), the mean score for students in the fall semester of first grade was at approximately the 44th percentile. By the spring of third grade, this difference had expanded significantly. Children living in high-poverty areas tend to fall further behind, regardless of their initial reading skill level.
>
> (p. 98)

If these children fall further and further behind "regardless of their initial reading skill level," how, then, can we help them by increasing their initial skill level at "real reading" through things like early phonemic awareness and overt instruction on decoding, as the report recommends? Clearly delivering better skills training won't solve the problem. And we have already seen that even good initial reading skills will not ensure that these children will be able to handle the demands of the complex varieties of academic language they will face in the later grades.

Finally, we reach the issues of racism and power. It is widely believed that such issues are "merely political," not directly relevant to reading and reading research. But the fact of the matter is that racism and power are just as much cognitive issues as they are political ones. Children will not identify with – they will even disidentify with – teachers and schools that they perceive as hostile, alien, or oppressive to their home-based identities (Holland and Quinn 1987). Indeed, I argue throughout this book that learning is all about identity and identification.

Claude Steele's (Steele 1992; Steele and Aronson 1995, 1998) groundbreaking work clearly demonstrates that in assessment contexts where issues of stereotypes based on race or gender are triggered, the performance of even quite adept learners seriously deteriorates (see Ferguson, 1998 for an important extension of Steele's work). Steele shows clearly that how people read when they are taking tests changes as their fear of falling victim to cultural stereotypes increases. In his work, highly educated college-age African-Americans and women do less well on math tests when, and only when, the tester, however subtly, triggers their fear of negative stereotypes (e.g. African-Americans are "less smart" or women are "no good at math"). Otherwise they perform as well as white males. To ignore these wider issues, while stressing such things as phonemic awareness, is to ignore not merely "politics," but what we know about learning and literacy as well.

In fact one can go further: given Steele's work, it is simply wrong to discuss reading assessment, intervention, and instruction without discussing the pervasive culture of inequality that deskills poor and minority children and its implications for different types of assessments, interventions, and instruction. This is an empirical point, not (only) a political one.

Thus, too, the research on African-Americans' changing fortunes on reading tests tells us, once again, that it is not early skills training that makes or breaks good readers. It is other factors. Throughout this chapter we have discussed the factor of mastering academic varieties of language. Here we see the additional factor of ensuring that people feel like they belong to and are a valued and accepted part of the social group within which their learning takes place. All learning is sensitive to issues of power, status, and solidarity, of course, but cultural processes like reading are particularly sensitive to these issues.

Children cannot feel they belong at school when their valuable home-based practices (like Leona's) are ignored, denigrated, and unused. They cannot feel like they belong when the real game is acquiring academic varieties of language, and they are given no help with this, as they watch other children get high assessments at school for what they have learned not at school but at home.

I mentioned in Chapter 2 that poverty and minority group status are not the only causes of children not flourishing in school. Some children, without disabilities and not from poor or minority homes, find academic varieties of language alienating. Indeed there are many adults who do. Sometimes these children find academic language alienating because their homes contain adults who do. Sometimes it is because instruction in school has made these varieties of language seem distant, irrelevant, and even frightening.

However, today, there may be another cause. Many children are exposed to language and other symbols connected to modern technologies and media (e.g. the Internet, video games, text messaging) that seem more compelling and motivating than school language. These forms of language are, in some cases, complex and fairly technical, so the issue is not just that academic language is technical or complex. These new technologies and media may well recruit forms of thinking, interacting, and valuing that are quite different from – and, again, more compelling and motivating than – those children find in today's schools. We will return to this issue in subsequent chapters.

4

SIMULATIONS AND BODIES

A paradox

In the second chapter we argued that learning to read works best as a cultural and not an instructed process. Indeed, we argued that this is true of all learning that is not natural in the sense of being supported by our human biology (as is the process of first-language acquisition). In this chapter I want to take up just one aspect of learning as a cultural process. We will take up other aspects in later chapters.

Learning does not work well when learners are forced to check their bodies at the school room door like guns in the old West. School learning is often about disembodied minds learning outside any context of decisions and actions. When people learn something as a cultural process their bodies are involved because cultural learning always involves having specific experiences that facilitate learning, not just memorizing words.

Traditionalists treat learning to read as if "read" was an intransitive verb. People just "read." But no one just reads; rather they read *something*. "Read" is a transitive verb; it requires an object, a thing being read. When people read they are always reading a specific type of text, whether this be a comic book, a recipe, a textbook, a legal brief, or a novel. Learning to read is about learning to read different types of text with real understanding. This is why learning to read and learning content can never really be separated. You can't read a book if the content of the book is meaningless to you.

I will argue that humans understand content, whether in a comic book or a physics text, much better when their understanding is embodied: that is, when they can relate that content to possible activities, decisions, talk, and dialogue. When people learn as a cultural process, whether this be cooking, hunting, or how to play video games, they learn through action and talk with others, not by memorizing words outside their contexts of application.

As we have seen, traditionalists think it's all about skills. They have stressed "phonics" (learning to relate letters and sounds) as the core problem in reading instruction to the exhaustion point. But they have ignored a much more important problem with learning to read – one crucial for children and adults who did not learn to read well early in life. This problem is actually quite a paradox.

Research has long shown that people with poor vocabularies are poor readers. This is, of course, especially true for reading texts written in specialist varieties of language. Research also shows that the only way poor readers can catch up in vocabulary is to do lots of reading, especially because teaching vocabulary out of the context of reading is not very effective. This is already paradoxical since these readers can't read well and, thus, are unlikely to do lots of reading, especially of texts filled with words they don't know. But the bigger paradox here is that reading is, in fact, not an especially good way to learn vocabulary. Consider, then, the two quotes below:

> the variety of contexts in which words can appropriately be used is so extensive, and the crucial nuances in meaning so constrained by context, that teaching word meanings in an abstract and decontextualized manner is essentially futile and potentially misleading . . .

> The only realistic chance students with poor vocabularies have to catch up to their peers with rich vocabularies requires that they engage in extraordinary amounts of independent reading. Furthermore, research findings are increasingly clear that opportunities for developing adequate reading skills are limited. In fact, the status quo in beginning reading instruction may be entirely insufficient to meet the reading and vocabulary needs of many diverse learners (Adams 1990; Liberman and Liberman 1990).
>
> (Baker *et al.* n.d.)

> It may be somewhat surprising to learn that most researchers agree that although students do learn word meanings in the course of reading connected text, the process seems to be fairly inefficient and not especially effective (Beck and McKeown, 1991). Beck and McKeown state that "research spanning several decades has failed to uncover strong evidence that word meanings are routinely acquired from context" (p. 799).
>
> (Gersten *et al.* 2001: p. 284)

So, poor readers cannot become good ones unless they improve their vocabularies. They can't improve their vocabularies unless they read a lot, but reading a lot is not a particularly effective way to increase one's vocabulary. So what, for heaven's sake, can be done? Are poor readers just fated to stay poor readers?

Think a minute what the above quotes imply about good readers. They have large vocabularies, especially for the specialist texts they can read, but they didn't get these large vocabularies by reading alone, since even reading a lot, in and of itself, is not an effective way for a large vocabulary to grow. So how did they get these vocabularies? The answer: they got these large vocabularies by having actually experienced the "worlds" to which these words refer.

Learning to read as an embodied process

One problem with learning vocabulary, which the quotes I offered above make clear, is that words do not have just general dictionary-like meanings. They have different and specific meanings in different situations where they are used and in different specialist domains that recruit them (Gee 1999a). This is true of the most mundane cases. For instance, notice the change in meaning in the word "coffee" in the following sentences which refer to different situations: "The coffee spilled, go get the mop" (coffee as liquid); "The coffee spilled, go get a broom" (coffee as grains); "The coffee spilled, stack it again" (coffee in cans).

Consider all the different meanings of "work" in the following sentences: "I'm going to work," "Relationships take work," "Joe is really working the system," "Bush's plan won't work," "I managed to work my point in," "I never dreamed I would work past the age of 65," "It was the work of God, not man," "Let's work this out before a fight starts." Many more could be added. Furthermore, these are all everyday (vernacular) uses of the word. The word "work" has a different meanings in the specialist domain of physics, for instance.

In the specialist domain of playing computer and video games, the term "power up" (as in "I just found a power up") has a general meaning – namely, any device that increases the player's (character's) health or powers – but knowing this general meaning is nearly worthless unless you can recognize and use power ups in specific situations in specific games. In different games, power ups look and function differently. So too with any word: knowing the general meaning is nearly worthless, unless you can recognize the word's applications in specific cases.

But here is our key: how does a gamer learn the specific meanings of a word like "power up"? Obviously, by playing games. How does any reader learn the specific meanings of any word. By playing the "games" the word is used in. Reading lots of texts may not be an effective way to learn what words mean specifically, but playing the games they are used in is. This is so because the games they are used in are what give them specific meanings.

What do I mean by the "games the word is used in"? Think of a word as a card that has a number of different "moves" you can make on it. You make these moves either in action (as you use words to think about what you are doing in certain ways) or in talk and dialogue with other people (itself a type of action). Thus the card for the word "work" has on it all the sorts of moves we saw above and more. But you cannot make a move unless you recognize the situation in the world of things or talk that the move refers to. For instance, you need to know whether this situation here and now is one where the move of using "work" in the sense of "work of God" can or cannot be made.

These word cards are yet more special. They allow "players" ("us") to consult the moves on the card and, by considering a specific situation we are in, make up a new but related meaning for the word, if the situation seems not to fit any of the moves on the card. Thus, knowing a number of moves on the card, someone could make up a meaning for "work" like "The work of childhood is learning to read." This is, in fact, a sentence that a traditionalist whom I will not name once uttered. She was trying to make meaning for a situation that was new: namely, attempting to make traditionalist reading professionals (like her) the key professionals in charge of early childhood, so as to push her specific agenda of how reading ought to be taught at home and in school. There is nothing special here; we humans do this all the time. She knew how to use her "work" card to construct a new, but properly related, meaning for the word. By the way, while I realize this meaning is perfectly meaningful, I disagree with her claim. In my view, the work of childhood is play.

Given that words work this way in the "real" world, it turns out we have a lot to learn from how people learn to read texts when they are playing video games. This is so because people learn how to read any given type of text by having played the games (that is, by having been in the situations) that the words and phrases in texts of that sort are used in. So far I have been using the word "game" metaphorically. I have meant to imply that you cannot, for example, learn what words in biology mean if you have never "played" biology (that is, experienced the situations in biology – situations involving action or talk – in which the words apply). In the case of video games we are dealing with a real game. The issues get very clear.

So let's look a moment at how gamers learn vocabulary about games and how they learn to read texts about games. What we learn here should be applicable to reading in other specialist domains. Computer and video games often contain lots of print and they come with manuals. It is notorious that young people don't read the manuals, but just play the game. While older people bemoan this fact as just one more indication that young people today don't read, these young people are making a very wise decision when they start by playing and not reading. The texts that come with games are very hard to understand unless and until one has some experience of playing the game – experience which, then, will give specific situated meanings to the language in the text.

Let me take the small booklet that comes with the innovative shooter game *Deus Ex* to use as an example of what I mean by saying that texts associated with video games are not lucid unless and until one has played the game. The book contains 20 small-sized pages, printed in double columns on each page. In these 20 pages, there are 199 references in bold that represent headings and subheadings (to take one small randomly chosen stretch of headings and subheadings that appears at the end of page 5 and the beginning of page 6: **Passive Readouts**, **Damage Monitor**, **Active Augmentation** & **Device Icons**, **Items-at-Hand**, **Information Screens**, **Note**, **Inventory**, **Inventory Management**, **Stacks**, **Nanokey ring**, **Ammunition**). Each of these 199 headings and subheadings is followed by text that gives information relevant to the topic and relates it to other information throughout the booklet. In addition, the booklet gives 53 keys on the computer keyboard an assignment to some function in the game, and these 53 keys are mentioned 82 times in the booklet in relation to the information contained in the 199 headings and subheadings. So, though the booklet is small, it is just packed with concise and relatively technical information.

Here is a typical piece of language from this booklet (p. 5):

> Your internal nano-processors keep a very detailed record of your condition, equipment and recent history. You can access this data at any time during play by hitting F1 to get to the Inventory screen or F2 to get to the Goals/Notes screen. Once you have accessed your information screens, you can move between the screens by clicking on the tabs at the top of the screen. You can map other information screens to hotkeys using Settings, Keyboard/Mouse.

This makes perfect sense at a literal level, but that just goes to show how worthless the literal level is. When you understand this sort of passage at only a literal level, you have only an illusion of understanding – one that quickly disappears as you try to relate the information in this passage to the hundreds of other important details in the booklet. Such literal understandings are precisely what kids who fuel the fourth-grade slump have. First of all, this passage means nothing real to you if you have no situated idea about what "nano-processors," "condition," "equipment," "history," "F1," "Inventory screen," "F2," "Goals/Notes screen" (and, of course, "Goals" and "Notes"), "information screens," "clicking," "tabs," "map," "hotkeys," and "Settings, Keyboard/Mouse" mean in and for playing games like *Deus Ex*.

Second, though you know literally what each of the sentences means, they raise a plethora of questions if you have no situated understandings of this game or games like it. For instance: is the same data (condition, equipment, and history) on both the Inventory screen and the Goals/Notes screen? If so, why is it on two different screens? If not, which type of information is on which screen and why? The fact that I can move between the screens by clicking on the tabs (but what do these tabs look like – will I recognize them?) suggests that some of this information is on one screen and some on the other. But, then, is my "condition" part of my Inventory or my Goals/Notes – doesn't seem to be either, but then what is my "condition" anyway? If I can map other information screens (and what are these?) to hotkeys using "Setting, Keyboard/Mouse," does this mean there is no other way to access them? How will I access them in the first place to assign them to my own chosen hotkeys? Can I click between them and the Inventory screen and the Goals/Notes screens by pressing on "tabs"? And so on and so forth – 20 pages is beginning to seem like a lot. Remember there are 199 different headings under which information like this is given at a brisk pace through the booklet.

Of course all these terms and questions can be defined and answered if you closely check and cross-check information over and over again throughout the little booklet. You can constantly turn the pages backwards and forwards. But once you have one set of links relating various items and actions in your mind, another drops out just as you need it and you're back to turning pages. Is the booklet poorly written? Not at all. In fact it is written just as well or poorly as any of a myriad of school-based texts in the content areas. It is, outside the practices in the domain from which it comes, just as meaningless, however much one could garner literal meanings from it with which to verbally repeat things or pass tests.

And, of course, too, you can utter something like "Oh, yea, you click on F1 [function key 1] to get to the Inventory screen and F2 to get to the Goals/Notes screen" and sound like you know something. The trouble is this: in the actual game, you can click on F2 and meditate on the screen you see at your leisure. Nothing bad will happen to you. However, you very often have to click on F1 and do something quickly in the midst of a heated battle. There's no "at your leisure" here. The two commands really don't function the same way in the game – they actually mean different things in terms of embodied and situated action – and they never really *just* mean "click F1, get screen." That's their general meaning, the one with which you can't really do anything useful until you know how to spell it out further in situation-specific terms in the game.

When you can spell out such information in situation-specific terms in the game, then the relationships of this information to the other hundreds of pieces of information in the booklet become clear and meaningful. And, of course, it is these relationships that are what really count if you are to understand the game as a system and, thus, play it at all well. *Now* you can read the book if you need to, to piece in missing bits of information, check on your understandings, solve a particular problem, or answer a particular question you have.

When I first read this booklet before playing *Deus Ex* (and I had played only one other shooter game before, a very different one) – yes, I, an overly academic Baby Boomer, made the mistake of trying to read the book first, despite my own theories about reading – I was sorely tempted to put the game on a shelf and forget about it. I was simply overwhelmed with details, questions, and confusions. When I started the game I kept trying to look up stuff in the booklet. But none of it was well enough understood to be found easily without continually re-searching for the same information. In the end, you have to just actively play the game and explore and try everything. Then, at last, the booklet makes good sense, but then too you don't need it all that much any more.

As we have discussed above, school requires, both in respect to oral and written language, academic varieties of language that are different from everyday vernacular oral language used in informal face-to-face conversations. These academic varieties of language are the sorts of language used in texts and discussions in science, math, social studies classes, and other content areas.

Academic language, just like the language in the *Deus Ex* booklet (which is, of course, a specialist variety of language itself), is not really lucid or meaningful if one has no embodied experiences within which to situate its meanings in specific ways. For example, consider the piece of academic language below from a geology textbook (taken from Martin 1990: p. 93):

> The destruction of a land surface by the combined effects of abrasion
> and removal of weathered material by transporting agents is called

erosion . . . The production of rock waste by mechanical processes and chemical changes is called weathering.

Again, one can certainly understand this at some literal word-by-word, sentence-by-sentence way. However, this is not "everyday" language. No one usually speaks this way at home around the table or at a bar having drinks with friends. But this language is filled with all the same problems the language of the *Deus Ex* booklet was for me when I had not lived through any experiences in terms of which I could situate its meanings. Without embodied experiences with which to cash out its meanings, all the above academic text will do – like the *Deus Ex* booklet did to me initially – is fill one with questions, confusion, and, perhaps, anger.

For example: I have no idea what the difference is between "abrasion" and "removal of weathered material by transporting agents," which I would have thought was one form of abrasion. What's a "transporting agent"? What's a "mechanical process"? I am not really clear on the difference between "mechanical processes," especially in regard to weather, and "chemical changes." And what chemicals are we talking about here – stuff in rain?

Since the first sentence is about "erosion" and the second about "weathering," I suppose these two things are connected in some important way – but how? They must (?) be two forms of "destruction of a land surface," given that this is the subject of the first sentence. But then I would have thought that producing "rock waste" was a way of building, not just destroying, land, since rock waste eventually turns into dirt (doesn't it?) and thus, I would have supposed, eventually into potentially fertile land. But then this is a geology text and they don't care about fertile land (or do they?). The word "land" here has a different range of situation-specific meanings than I am familiar with.

Of course I can turn the pages of the book back and forth clarifying all these points. After all, these two sentences are meant to be definitions, though not of the words "erosion" and "weathering" in everyday terms, but in specialist terms. And, of course, I do need to know that they *are* definitions and I may not even know that if I have had little experience of specialists trying to define terms in explicit and operational ways so as to lessen the sort of ambiguity and vagueness that is more typical of everyday talk. Since they are definitions, they are linked and cross-linked to a myriad of other terms, descriptions, and explanations throughout the book and I can follow this tangled trail across the pages, back and forth, losing bits of the connections just as I need them and page-turning yet again.

However, once I have experienced the sorts of embodied images, actions, and tasks that engage geologists – including their ways of talking and debating, their reasons for doing so, their interests, norms, and values – then the text is lucid and useful. Confusion, frustration, and anger disappear. However, given such understanding, everybody would pass the test and we couldn't fail half the class and reward a small set of "winners", i.e. people who can repeat back verbal details they remember well when they don't fully understand them in any practical way.

The argument is this, then: learning to read in a way that allows people more than a literal understanding, that does not fuel the fourth-grade slump and create poor readers, requires that people "play" in a domain in such a way that they can give situation-specific meanings to the styles of language associated with that domain. The phonics debate is wildly misplaced. Of course people must learn to decode. Different learners learn to decode in different ways. The emphasis in debates about learning to read ought to be on how every learner can learn reading as a cultural process. Once this discussion is started, we can, among many other things, talk about how learning to decode works in such cultural learning processes.

Identity and decoding

Decoding print – that is, relating letters to sounds – is a good example of a skill that in and of itself doesn't have any real meaning. Neither sounds nor letters themselves have any meanings. We decode so we can get to more meaningful tasks like understanding and arguing with a text. It is easy to believe, as the traditionalists do, that the best way to learn such skills is to practice them over and over again out of any meaningful contexts. However, many children learn to decode print as part of larger activities which do have deep meaning and value to the children.

I want to put the matter this way, using a metaphor: many children learn decoding and other seemingly meaningless skills as part and parcel of learning and acting in "games" they value. Of course I am using the word "game" metaphorically again here. Let me take a moment to say just how I want to use this word. When you are playing a game, you have to know what moves count as playing the game and what moves do not count. For example, in chess some moves are "legal" in the sense that they count as acceptable moves in the game. Other moves are not legal. You aren't playing chess if you don't make legal moves. No one will recognize you as playing chess if you don't make legal moves.

Now let me put another term into the mix, the word "identity," used somewhat metaphorically as well. When you are playing chess properly, that is, making legal moves, I will say you are acting out an *identity* as a chess player. Others recognize you as an appropriate chess player and you recognize yourself as being an appropriate chess player as well. None of this says you are a good chess player, just that you are acting like an appropriate ("legal") one because you are making legal moves.

I want to say that a child or an adult is engaging in a "game" whenever they are taking on a specific sort of identity defined by certain "moves": that is, certain sorts of actions and interactions that define them as playing a certain sort of role. Thus, in this sense, I will say that I am playing a game when I am being an academic, because I need to make certain sorts of moves to get recognized as being an academic, For example, I have to write and talk in a certain way. In my earlier work I have used the term "Discourse" with a capital "D" for this sense of the term "game" here (Gee 1990, 1996, 1999a).

A policeman is playing a game when he or she is playing out his or her role or

46

identity as a policeman of a certain sort. The policeman has to make certain sorts of moves (that is, say or do certain sorts of things in certain ways) to get recognized as being a policeman of a certain sort (e.g. a "tough cop"). When a child is trying to act like a scientist in his or her science classroom, he or she is, in this sense, playing a specific sort of game. There are moves the child needs to know how to make if he or she is to get accepted as playing the role of a particular type of scientist, at least in this classroom.

Of course in this sense of "game" we are always playing one game or another. We are always acting in terms of some identity or another. I know that some people will object to using "game" in this way. They will say (correctly) that being a policeman is "no game," but a serious matter. But all I want to stress, without trivializing the work of policemen, is that policemen need to know what "moves" they can and cannot make so as to be recognized as legitimate policemen, and indeed policemen of different types (which require different types of moves). I need to know what moves I can and cannot make to get recognized (for better or worse) as an academic of a certain sort. A child needs to know what moves he or she can make to get recognized as a "good student" in Mrs Smith's first-grade class.

Of course, the games we play in "real" life are not like chess. The rules aren't always clear and they are clearer in some cases than others. People can disagree over whether certain moves are appropriate or not. Some people may think I write like an academic and recognize me in this identity. Others may not. And I and others might dispute the matter – might argue that academics can write in ways other people think they shouldn't. There may be real disagreements about what moves make one recognizable as a "real" Native American, for example. But those are the sorts of games we humans play. We fight over the rules and the application of the rules, much like children playing real games in the school yard.

So, back to my claim that many children learn to decode print as part and parcel of learning and acting in "games" they value. For example, consider Brian again, the little boy we discussed in the last chapter. Brian learned to decode and to read inside three specific games (three specific identities connected to specific sorts of moves, i.e. ways of acting, interacting, and valuing).

First was the game of playing out the identity of being a member of a specific family and its social group. Given his particular family, he acted and interacted in specific ways with a massive number of artifacts that supported emergent literacy, phonemic awareness, and, most importantly, the sorts of verbal abilities we discussed in the last chapter under the rubric of "early prototypes of academic language." Early forms of specialist languages appeared in his non-narrative books and DVDs and in some of the talk his family did with him around his major interests (e.g. trains, games, Pokémon). Thus becoming a "person like us" (an identity as a member of a family of a certain sort) involved early commitment to certain forms of language that would and did facilitate later success in reading at school. Learning to play the game of being a member of a family of a certain sort taught Brian certain "moves," some of which turned out to be skills that transferred to school.

Second, Brian brought his emerging home-based identity and the moves associated with it to his very active efforts to master the Pokémon universe via the Internet, cards, figures, and later video games. Brian wanted to know how to make the right moves in the Pokémon universe. As we saw in the second chapter, there are hundreds of Pokémon with multisyllabic names, but Brian wanted to be able to recognize and decode, and ultimately write, their names. This experience began his decoding career, though in a very meaningful context. For Brian, Pokémon names were not decontextualized. They always existed very much within the whole Pokémon universe, as well as within the activities and dialogue in which he engaged in regard to that universe. In this universe, Brian took on the identity of a Pokémon fan, even expert. Pokémon was not just a video game, it was a world: a larger game composed of many subgames (video games, television shows, books, etc.). But he approached the Pokémon universe under the influence of his emerging identity as a member of a family of a certain sort, an identity which we have argued had connections to identities he would see later in school. His family encouraged him to consume Pokémon in active ways connected to school-based values and ways with words.

Third, Brian took on a specific identity at school. It is important to see that for Brian school involved taking on an identity as a certain type of student – one affiliated with school and ready to be a literate person of a certain sort – an identity that was deeply connected to the two other identities we discussed. Brian wanted to make the right moves to be seen as a student of a certain sort by his teacher and parents. His emerging school-based identity was connected to his identity as a "person like us" that was part and parcel of becoming a member of his family. It was connected as well to his identity as a Pokémon fan (expert) who wanted and had started to read specialist language in the Pokémon world.

Brian received some good early instruction in phonics. But long before the teacher had finished the book he decoded, soon at several grade levels above his grade. He brought an iceberg of understanding to class. To pretend that the school phonics instruction – something which contributed only to the tip of that iceberg – was responsible for him becoming a reader is a crime. It is yet worse to pretend that the tip can make up for the whole iceberg for those children who come to school without it.

For Brian, learning to decode was not "decontextualized." It was not, in fact, separated from meaningful and value-laden action, interaction, and dialogue, as it is for so many children in school. Rather, it was fully contextualized within the games Brian played to be a recognizable member of a certain sort of family, a recognizable Pokémon fan, and a recognizable student of a certain sort. These identities all tied together to support not just Brian's early reading, but his affiliation with academic forms of language.

So I have used the words "game" and "identity" here. I have done so because I am arguing that learning to read, or any learning for that matter, is not all about skills. It is about learning the right moves in embodied interactions in the real world or virtual worlds, moves that get one recognized as "playing the game":

that is, enacting the right sort of identity for a given situation (e.g. science class in middle school).

Meaning, perceiving, and acting

I have argued that reading – as in reading the *Deus Ex* text – is an embodied process. That is, we read through simulations of experiences we have had. I read the *Deus Ex* manual by recalling images and actions from the game world.

I want now to briefly survey current work in cognitive science that supports this viewpoint. We will see here that, at bottom, how we comprehend oral language and written language is the same. For humans, language, perception (including emotion), and action in the world are all tightly connected together.

It used to be, and still is in some quarters, a standard view in psychology that the meaning of a word is some general concept in the head that can be spelled out in something like a definition. For example, the word "bachelor" might be represented by a complex concept in the head that the following definition would capture: "a male who is not married."

However, today there are accounts of language and thinking that are quite different. Consider, for instance, these two quotes from some recent work in cognitive psychology: "comprehension is grounded in perceptual simulations that prepare agents for situated action" (Barsalou 1999a: p. 77); and "to a particular person, the meaning of an object, event, or sentence is what that person can do with the object, event, or sentence" (Glenberg 1997: p. 3). These two quotes are from work that is part of a "family" of related viewpoints. For want of a better name, we might call the family "situated cognition studies," which means that these viewpoints all believe that thinking is connected to, and changes across, actual situations and is not usually a process of applying abstract generalizations, definitions, or rules (e.g. Barsalou 1999a, b; Brown *et al.* 1989; Clark 1997, 2003; Engestrom *et al.* 1999; Gee 1992; Glenberg 1997; Glenberg and Robertson 1999; Hutchins 1995; Latour 1999; Lave 1996; Lave and Wenger 1991; Wertsch 1998; Wenger 1998). While there are differences among the different members of the family, they share the viewpoint that language is tied to *people's experiences of situated action in the material and social world*. Furthermore, these experiences are stored in the mind/brain, not in terms of language but in something like dynamic images tied to perception both of the world and of our own bodies, internal states, and feelings: "Increasing evidence suggests that perceptual simulation is indeed central to comprehension" (Barsalou 1999a: p. 74).

Let me use a metaphor to make clear what this viewpoint means. Not surprisingly, at this point I will use video games as the source of my metaphor. Video games like *Deus Ex*, *Half-Life*, *Age of Mythology*, *Rise of Nations*, or *Neverwinter Nights* involve a visual and auditory world in which the player manipulates a virtual character. Such games often come with editors or other sorts of software with which the player can make changes to the game world or even build a new game world. The player can make a new landscape, a new set of buildings, or new characters. The player can set up the world so that certain sorts of actions are allowed or disallowed. The player is building a new world, but is doing so by using, but modifying, the original visual images (really the code for them) that came with the game. One simple example of this is the way in which players can build new skateboard parks in a game like *Tony Hawk Pro Skater*. The player must place ramps, trees, grass, poles, and other things in space in such a way that he or she or other players can manipulate their virtual characters to skateboard the park in a fun and challenging way.

So imagine the mind works in a similar way. We have experiences in the world, including things we have experienced only in the media. Let us use as an example experiences of weddings. These are our raw materials, like the game with which the gamer starts. Based on these experiences, we can build a simulated model of a wedding. We can move around as a character in the model as ourselves, imagining our role in the wedding, or we can "play" other characters at the wedding (e.g. the minister), imagining what it is like to be that person. The model we build is not "neutral." Rather the model is meant to take a perspective on weddings. It foregrounds certain aspects of weddings that we take as important or salient. It backgrounds other elements that we think are less important or less salient. It leaves some things out altogether.

However, we do not build just one wedding model simulation and store it away once and for all in our minds. No: what we do, rather, is build different simulations on the spot for different specific contexts we are in. In a given situation or conversation involving weddings, we build a model simulation that fits that context and helps us to make sense of it. Out models are specially built to help us make sense of the specific situations we are in, conversations we are having, or texts we are reading. In one case we might build a model that foregrounds weddings as fun, blissful, and full of potential for a long and happy future. In another case we might build a model that foregounds weddings as complex, stressful, and full of potential for problematic futures.

We build our model simulations to help us make sense of things. Sometimes this does not work all that well. For example, every time I see or hear about the sport of cricket, I build model simulations based on my experiences of baseball. I build different ones on different occasions, since they never seem to work well to make really good sense of what I am seeing or hearing. If I ever got deeper and better experiences of cricket, I could make better models. Furthermore, I could then use those experiences, if I had enough of them, to build more direct simulations of cricket worlds – ones less influenced by baseball. I might even be able to use these to understand baseball in a new way by comparing it to some specific cricket model.

We also build our model simulations to help us prepare for action in the world. We can act in the model and test out what consequences follow, before we act in the real world. We can role-play another person in the model and try to see what motivates their actions or what might follow from them before we respond to them in the real world. In fact, humans tend to want to understand objects and words in terms of their "affordances" for actions. Take something as simple as a glass:

> The meaning of the glass to you, at [a] particular moment, is in terms of the actions available. The meaning of the glass changes when different constraints on action are combined. For example, in a noisy room, the glass may become a mechanism for capturing attention (by tapping it with a spoon), rather than a mechanism for quenching thirst.
>
> (Glenberg 1997: p. 41)

Faced with the word "glass" in a text or a glass in a specific situation, the word or object takes on a specific meaning or significance based not just on the model simulation we build, but also on the actions with the glass that we see as salient in the model. In one case, we build a model simulation in which the glass is "for drinking"; in another it is "for ringing like a bell to get attention"; in another it is a precious heirloom in a museum that is "not for touching." Our models stress affordances for action so that they can prepare us to act or not act in given ways in the real world.

We think and prepare for action with and through our model simulations. They are what we use to give meaning to our experiences in the world and to prepare us for action in the world. They are what we use to give meaning to words and sentences. But they are not language. Furthermore, since they are representations of experience (including feelings, attitudes, embodied positions, and various sorts of foregroundings and backgroundings of attention), they are not just "information" or "facts." Rather they are value-laden, perspective-taking "games in the mind."

Of course talking about simulations in the mind is a metaphor that, like all metaphors, is incorrect if pushed too far (see Barsalou, 1999b for how a similar metaphor can be cashed out and corrected by a consideration of a more neurally realistic framework for "perception in the mind"). What I want to stress about our model simulations are two things: (a) they are specially built and we make them on the spot to help us make sense of and act in specific contexts or with specific texts; (b) they are not "neutral," but capture a given perspective or viewpoint, foregrounding some things and backgrounding others, though our perspective or viewpoint changes in different contexts. We can, of course, run simulations that reflect perspectives and values we ourselves don't believe in or even value by running a simulation from the perspective of someone else. This is how to under-stand people and texts we don't like.

So meaning is not about general definitions in the head. It is about building specific game-like models (wherein we can act or role-play other people's actions) for specific contexts. Even words that seem so clearly to have clear definitions, like the word "bachelor" that we used as an example at the beginning of this section, do not. Meaning is not about definitions, it is about simulations of experience. For example, what model simulation(s) would you bring to a situation where someone said of a woman, "She's the bachelor of the group"? I would build a simulation in which the woman was attractive, at or a little over marriageable age, perhaps a bit drawn to the single life and afraid of marriage, but open to the possibilities. I would see myself as acting in various ways towards the woman and see her responding in various ways. The fact that the woman is not an "unmarried man" does not stop me from giving meaning to this utterance. You, having had different experiences than me, would form a different sort of simulation. Perhaps the differences between my simulation and yours are big, perhaps they are small. They are small if you and I have had similar experiences in life and larger if we have not.

Of course if we were in a situation in which we didn't just hear about the woman but saw her, we would build our simulation to reflect what we see and know. Nonetheless, there is much room left for "gaming" – for running the simulation in various directions to make sense of what is going on, to try to predict what may happen, to make decisions about what we should say or do, or to make decisions about what the meaning is of what others have said and done.

Children play games early in life to prepare themselves for real life. It turns out we all play games in our heads to prepare us for action and decision in the real world. Our experiences in life allow us to build "wedding games" in order to think, talk, and act in regard to weddings and things related to weddings. When we use these models to act in the real world, we can, then, change the wedding game, that is, the real-world experiences we or others have of weddings. Our models and the real world are always interacting with each other. The world offers us raw materials for our simulations and our simulations cause us to act in the real world in ways that change it to better resemble or model simulations.

Once we see how important being able to simulate experiences in our mind is to comprehending oral and written language, we can see the importance of supplying all children in schools with the range of necessary experiences with which they can build good and useful simulations for understanding things like science. We can also see a potential role for things like video games that allow people to experience and act in new worlds.

Language and perspective-taking

We have, thus far, stressed the close connections between meaning and experience. But our experiences of talk and dialogue with other people are equally important as our experiences of action in the world. We not only give meaning to language by building model simulations of our experiences that capture certain perspectives on that experience, but language itself is built to allow people to take and communicate different perspectives.

Consider, in this regard, the following quote from Michael Tomasello's recent book *The cultural origins of human cognition* (1999):

> the perspectival nature of linguistic symbols, and the use of linguistic symbols in discourse interaction in which different perspectives are

explicitly contrasted and shared, provide the raw material out of which the children of all cultures construct the flexible and multi-perspectival – perhaps even dialogical – cognitive representations that give human cognition much of its awesome and unique power.

(p. 163)

Let's briefly unpack what this means. From the point of view of the theory Tomasello is developing, the words and grammar of a human language exist to allow people to take and communicate alternative perspectives on experience (see also Hanks 1996). That is, words and grammar exist to give people alternative ways to view one and the same state of affairs. Language is not about conveying neutral or "objective" information; rather it is about communicating perspectives on experience and action in the world, often in contrast to alternative and competing perspectives: "We may then say that linguistic symbols are social conventions for inducing others to construe, or take a perspective on, some experiential situation" (Tomasello 1999: p. 118).

This is not surprising, since we have argued already that we humans give meaning to language by running simulations of our previous experiences. Now we see that language is already built to convey perspectives on experience, not to offer neutral viewpoints detached from how people actually see things. Human language is built to support human thinking, both of which are perspectival.

Let me give some examples of what it means to say that words and grammar are not primarily about giving and getting information, but, rather, about giving and getting different perspectives on experience. I open Microsoft's website: are products I can download from the site without paying a price for them "free" or are they being "exchanged" for having bought other Microsoft products (e.g. Windows)? Saying "The download was free because I already owned Windows" takes a different perspective on the same sort of experience than "The download was paid for when I bought Windows" does.

If I use the grammatical construction "Microsoft's new operating system is loaded with bugs," I take a perspective in which Microsoft is less agentive and responsible than if I use the grammatical construction "Microsoft has loaded its new operating system with bugs."

Another example: do I say that a child who is using multiple cues to give meaning to a written text (i.e. using some decoding along with picture and context cues) is "reading" (as Whole Language people do), or do I say that she is "not really reading, but engaged in emergent literacy" (as pro-phonics traditionalists say – for these people the child is only "really reading" when she is decoding all the words in the text and not using non-decoding cues for word recognition). In this case, contending camps actually fight over what perspective on experience the term "reading" or "really reading" ought to name. For any speaker the word always names some perspective on experience (though, as we have seen, words can take on different meanings, and thus express different perspectives in different situations of use; think of a word as a card with different situation-specific "moves" on it, each of which involves a particular perspective). In the end, the point is that no wording is ever neutral or just "the facts." All wordings – given the very nature of language – are perspectives on experience that exist alongside of competing perspectives in the grammar of the language and in actual social interactions.

How do children learn how words and grammar line up to express particular perspectives on experience? Here, interactive, intersubjective dialogue with more advanced peers and adults appears to be crucial. In such dialogue, children come to see, from time to time, that others have taken a different perspective on what is being talked about than they themselves have. At a certain developmental level, children have the capacity to distance themselves from their own perspectives and (internally) simulate the perspectives the other person is taking, thereby coming to see how words and grammar come to express those perspectives (in contrast to the way in which different words and grammatical constructions express competing perspectives).

Later, in other interactions, or in thinking to oneself, the child can re-run such simulations and imitate the perspective-taking the more advanced peer or adult has done by using certain sorts of words and grammar. Through such simulations and imitative learning, children learn to use the symbolic means that other persons have used to share attention with them: "In imitatively learning a linguistic symbol from other persons in this way, I internalize not only their communicative intention (their intention to get me to share their attention) but also the specific perspective they have taken" (Tomasello 1999: p. 128).

Tomasello also points out (1999: pp. 129–30) – in line with our previous discussion that the world and texts are assigned meanings in the same way – that children come to use objects in the world as symbols at the same time (or with just a bit of a time lag) as they come to use linguistic symbols as perspective-taking devices on the world. Furthermore, they learn to use objects as symbols (to assign them different meanings encoding specific perspectives in different contexts) in the same way they learn to use linguistic symbols. In both cases, the child simulates in her head and later imitates in her words and deeds the perspectives her interlocutor must be taking on a given situation, by using certain words and certain forms of grammar or by treating certain objects in certain ways. Thus meaning for words, grammar, and objects comes out of intersubjective dialogue and interaction: "human symbols [are] inherently social, intersubjective, and perspectival" (Tomasello 1999: p. 131).

Perspective-taking and moral reasoning

It turns out, not surprisingly when one thinks about it, that there is a deep connection between morality and language as perspective-taking learned in dialogue with others. Such connections have been drawn since at least Piaget's 1932 book *The moral judgment of the child*. In regard to moral reasoning, however, the sort of dialogue that appears to be most important is not that between the child and more advanced peers or adults, but rather dialogue with and between equals.

For Piaget moral reasoning is not about following rules dictated by authority figures, "but rather it is about empathizing with other persons and being able to see and feel things from their point of view" (Tomasello 1999: p. 180). Piaget argued that what was most crucial for the development of moral reasoning was *discourse interactions with peers* (and not authority figures). Moral reasoning evolves from children's empathetic engagement with others as they attempt to transcend their own personal perspectives, take the perspectives of their interlocutors, and put themselves "in their shoes":

> Rules carrying rewards and punishments from adults do not foster this experience, and indeed in many ways impede it. It is in social interaction and discourse with others who are equal in terms of knowledge and power that children are led to go beyond rule-following and to engage with other moral agents who have thoughts and feelings like their own (see also Damon 1983). Note again that it is not the content of the language that is crucial – although some of children's moral development surely does consist of explicit and verbalized principles passed to them from others – but the process of engaging another mind in discourse dialogically.
>
> (Tomasello 1999: pp. 180–1)

In interaction with more advanced peers and adults, children learn to use language to take new perspectives on experience, but they may not question those perspectives very deeply (nor deeply enough to compare and contrast them to their own previous perspectives to see whether they really do want to give up their own perspectives or not). In dialogue with equals, children appear to compare and contrast perspectives more deeply and reflectively, learning thereby not only how to take particular perspectives through language, but also how to reason about such perspectives and perspective-taking.

I want to stress that this view of the connections between moral reasoning and peer-based dialogue are empirically supported. A variety of studies have shown that, in peer–peer discourse, children are less likely simply to defer to the authority of the other's viewpoint, more likely to seek some rational way to deal with differing viewpoints and perspectives, and more likely to actually change their own viewpoint for reasons they understand (Piaget 1932; Damon 1983; Dunn 1988).

Kruger (1992) is an interesting study that shows the importance of peer–peer interaction (that is, interaction among equals), as against interaction with adult authority figures. Kruger (1992; see also Kruger and Tomasello 1986) assessed seven- and eleven-year-old children on their moral reasoning skills as measured by the complexity and sophistication of their argumentation about a story in which there was a question about how to divide up rewards among a group of people who had made different contributions to a task. Some of the children then had further discussions with a peer, while other children had further discussions with their mothers. After the discussions, the children's moral reasoning skills were again assessed. Children who had carried out discussion with a peer made greater gains than did the children who had carried out the discussion with their mother.

Kruger discovered that in the peer groups much more reflective discourse (that is, discourse in which one person talks explicitly about the view expressed by the other) took place and that such reflective discourse was correlated with the progress individual children made. In reflective discourse children make comments or ask questions about the beliefs and desires of others or themselves: e.g. "Does she think I like X?" or "I don't want her to want my X" (Tomasello 1999: p. 181). As they engage in such talk, children simulate what other people have said and done in relation to their own words, desires, perspectives, and deeds, thereby seeing what the world and they themselves look like from the perspective of the other. Interestingly, young children often think that they themselves have said or done what was actually said or done by a peer with whom they collaborated (Foley and Ratner 1997).

We see here, again, the potential importance of modern technologies like video games. Such games, especially when played as multiplayer games, allow a group of peers to problem-solve collaboratively, through talk and action, in new (virtual) worlds. These worlds can be – and they often are even in current games – constructed to allow for moral dialogue and reflection. But here such dialogue and reflection take place inside the situations that have triggered them, not detached from them. We all know it is easy to take a high moral, even moralistic, stance when one is not actually faced with any need to act, feel, or make decisions in an actual situation.

Imagine the teenager faced, in a game, with the decision whether or not to get an abortion, realizing that she will play the rest of the game as a single mother and not part, say, of the other kids' activities, which are no longer really appropriate for a parent. For her there are now two possible ways to look at the future of her game. In this situation moral reflections on abortion become situated. She will also have to think about what it means if she makes one choice for her character in the game, but feels she would make a different choice in "real" life. Do some people's choices in "real" life get made because they cannot imagine vividly enough the future consequences of their choice? Video games are nothing if not vivid.

5

LEARNING AND GAMING

Introduction

Several times thus far I have used how people learn when they play video games as an example of good learning. In the last chapter I made an analogy between video games and the sorts of mental simulations through which we humans think and learn. In this chapter I want to treat the issue of learning and video games more directly. Good video games have a great deal to teach us about how to facilitate learning, even in domains outside games, even in school (Gee 2003). Good video games are complex, challenging, and long; they can take 50 or more hours to finish. If a game cannot be learned well, then it will fail to sell well, and the company that makes it is in danger of going broke. Shortening and dumbing games down is not an option, since most avid players don't want short or easy games. Thus, if only to sell well, good games have to incorporate good learning principles in virtue of which they get themselves well learned. Game designers build on each other's successes and, in a sort of Darwinian process, good games come to reflect yet better and better learning principles.

The learning principles that good games incorporate are by no means unknown to researchers in the learning sciences. In fact current research on learning supports the sorts of learning principles that good games use, though these principles are often exemplified in games in particularly striking ways (for a survey and citations of the literature, see Gee 2003). However, many of these principles are much better reflected in good games than they are in today's schools, where we also ask young people to learn complex and challenging things. With the current return in our schools to skill-and-drill and curricula driven by standardized tests, good learning principles have, more and more, been left on the cognitive scientist's laboratory bench and, I will argue, inside good computer and video games.

Game design involves modeling human interactions with and within complex virtual worlds, including learning processes as part and parcel of these inter-actions. This is, in fact, not unlike design research in educational psychology where researchers model new forms of interaction connected to learning in class-rooms (complex worlds, indeed), study such interactions to better understand how and why they lead to deep learning, and then ultimately disseminate them across a great many classrooms (see, for example, the chapters in Kelly 2003).

There are many different types of computer and video games, such as shooters (e.g. *Deus Ex, Return to Castle Wolfenstein, Unreal II: The Awakening*), squad-based shooters (e.g. *Tom Clancy's Ghost Recon, Operation Flashpoint: Cold War Crisis*), adventure games (e.g. *The Longest Journey, Siberia*), simulations (e.g. *The Sims, SimCity 4, Black and White*), role-playing games (e.g. *Baldur's Gate II: Shadows of Amn, The Elder Scrolls III: Morrowind, Star Wars: Knights of the Old Republic*), real-time strategy games (e.g. *Age of Empires, Age of Mythology, Rise of Nations*), action/arcade games (e.g. *Sonic Adventure 2 Battle, Super Smash Brothers, Sly Cooper and Thievius Raccoonus*), and a good number of other types.

This chapter discusses one real-time strategy game, namely *Rise of Nations*. Hereafter I will refer to real-time strategy games as "RTS games" and to *Rise of Nations* as "*RoN*." RTS games are among the most complex and demanding of computer and video games. In such games, players play a civilization of their choosing – a civilization for which they must make a myriad of decisions. They send their citizens out to gather resources (e.g. food, wood, minerals, gold) and use these resources to build domestic and military buildings and engage in various forms of research. In these buildings they can train soldiers and other sorts of people (e.g. leaders, priests, scientists, and/or professors), as well as build military and other sorts of apparatus. As they gather and build, they can advance to different ages, allowing their civilization to achieve higher levels of complexity and sophistication. All the while they must go to war against or engage in diplomacy with other civilizations.

All of this is done in real time. While the player builds up his or her civilization, other players (or the computer representing other players) are building up theirs as well. Players must decide when to attack or engage in diplomacy. Victory may come to the swift: that is, to those who attack early (a strategy called "rushing"), or to those who wait and patiently build up (a strategy called "turtling").

RoN is one of the best RTS games ever made (along with such excellent games as *Civilization III, StarCraft, WarCraft III: Reign of Chaos*, and *Age of Mythology*). *RoN* allows the player to play one of 18 civilizations (e.g. Aztecs, Bantu, British, Chinese, Egyptians, Maya, Nubians, Russians, Spanish), each with different advantages and disadvantages. The player can play against one to seven opponents (other real people or the computer playing other civilizations). Players can move through eight ages from the Ancient Age to the Information Age through various intervening ages such as the Medieval Age, the Gunpowder Age, and the Enlightenment Age. Like all RTS games, *RoN* involves players learning well over a hundred different commands, each connected to decisions that need to be made, as they move through a myriad of different menus (there are 102 commands on the abridged list that comes printed on a small sheet enclosed with the game). Furthermore, players must operate at top speed if they are to keep up with skilled opponents who are building up as they are. *RoN* involves a great deal of micromanagement and decision-making under time pressure.

This chapter is based on an analysis of my own learning and personal inter-actions with the game as a game player. Learning differs from individual to individual, so we need to base our discussions of learning around actual cases of actual people learning. This is not to say, however, that no generality exists here. How any one of us learns throws light, both by comparison and contrast, on how others learn. Learning is not infinitely variable and there are patterns and principles to be discovered – patterns and principles that ultimately constitute a theory of learning. Indeed, what I am offering here is a case study meant to offer suggestions for a theory of how deep learning works (see also Barsalou 1999a, b; diSessa 2000; Glenburg 1997; Glenburg and Robertson 1999). In the end, I hope to convince you that today's young people often see deeper and better forms of learning going on in the games they play than in the schools they attend.

Though some of the information below is personal, I intend and hope that readers will think about the comparisons and contrasts of my learning experience with *RoN* to the sorts of learning that goes on in schools. Ironically perhaps, a Baby Boomer trying to learn a modern computer or video game is not in some respects unlike a child in school trying to learn science or math. Both parties are being asked to learn something new and in some respects alien to their taken-for-granted ways of thinking.

Preparation for learning: before *RoN*

By the time I started up *RoN* I had played lots of computer and video games. They had taught me new ways of learning and new things about myself as a learner (Gee 2003). However, I had not had good experiences with RTS games. I felt overwhelmed by their many details and by the pressure of competing in real time. I had watched my twin brother play RTS games at a high level and was amazed by the number of details he had mastered and the speed with which he had acted and thought in the games. I had watched my seven-year-old son play the wonderful *Age of Mythology* and was stunned that he and his friends could play such a complicated game so well. Far from giving me confidence, these experiences just made me think that I was not suited for the micromanagement and on-the-spot decision-making RTS games demanded. In regard to RTS games, I was an "at-risk" learner – at risk for failing to be able to learn and enjoy these sorts of games.

Though timid about RTS games, when *WarCraft III* came out I tried it, prodded by my brother who loved the game. I made some progress in the single-player campaign, but eventually found the game "too hard." We should pause a moment though at this phrase "too hard." *WarCraft III* is a superbly designed game. In fact, it is well designed to get itself learned. So when I say it was "too hard," what I really mean is that I failed to engage with it in a way that fully recruited its solid design and learning principles. Good games are never really "too hard." They fail, for some players, either because their designers did not use good learning principles or because players have, for one reason or another, failed to engage the good learning principles that are built into the games.

So something has to come even before good learning principles. What has to come before is *motivation for an extended engagement* with the game. Without a commitment to an extended engagement no deep learning of a complex domain can happen (diSessa 2000). So what made me motivated to offer such extended engagement to *RoN* and not earlier to *WarCraft III?* Well, as good as *WarCraft III* is, *RoN* is yet better at allowing newcomers to learn it. But, more importantly, and ironically perhaps, my "failure" at *WarCraft III* motivated me to try *RoN.* I had liked *WarCraft III.* It had made me feel that RTS games were important and worth playing. Though I had had limited success with the game, I had had some small success that made me feel that at another time and place, perhaps, I would do better. It had led me to read about RTS games and reflect on them. *WarCraft III*, it turned out – though I realized this fully only when I started *RoN* – had *prepared me for future learning* (Bransford and Schwartz 1999) of RTS games. When I started *RoN*, I realized that I already knew something – somewhat more than I had thought. I felt I had a small foot up.

In a school setting, my experience with *WarCraft III* would simply have been seen as a failure as I received my low or failing grade. In reality it was not a failure, but an important precursor for later learning. My experience with *WarCraft III* is what I will call, following the work of Stan Goto (2003), a "horizontal" learning experience. "Vertical" learning experiences are cases where a learner makes lots of incremental progress on a scale from low skills to high skills, as if moving up a ladder. "Horizontal" learning experiences are those where one does not make a lot of progress up the ladder of skills, but stays on the initial rungs awhile, exploring them and getting to know what some of the rungs are and what the ladder looks like. Horizontal experiences look like mucking around, but they are really ways of getting your feet wet, getting used to the water, and getting ready, eventually, to jump in and go swimming. They may, in one form or another, be essential to learning, or at least essential for learners who are "at risk."

So is there a contradiction in saying that when I started *RoN* I was still an "at-risk" learner, but that my experiences with *WarCraft III* were important preparation for future learning? No. All that my being "at risk" meant, in the end, was that if *RoN* had failed to reward my preparation for future learning (the future was here with *RoN*) or had been a bad learning experience – a real failure – then I may have given up on RTS games forever, assuming I was too "dumb" to learn them. This is all "at risk" needs to mean in schools too, though there it often means giving "at-risk" learners a special dumbed-down curriculum meant to catch them up on "basic skills" – a curriculum that all too often is a bad learning experience for these students.

Computer and video games have a built-in advantage in the creation of motivation for an extended engagement. Human beings feel that their bodies and minds extend, in a rather intimate way, to the area around them over which they have direct control, usually a fairly small area (Clark 2003). Thus, as I type, I feel that my keyboard and mouse are almost like extensions of my fingers, just as blind people often feel that their cane is an extension of their hand. The space close around my body seems to be connected to it in such a way that I can feel that it is being "invaded" by others.

When humans can manipulate something at a distance, for example controlling with a keyboard a far-away robot seen on a screen, they get an uncanny feeling that their minds and bodies have been vastly extended (Clark 2003; Goldberg 2001). When people are playing a computer or video game they are manipulating a character (or many different things in an RTS game) at a distance in a very fine-grained way – in this case a virtual distance. They feel that their minds and bodies have been extended into this virtual world. This process appears to allow players to identify powerfully with the virtual character or characters they are playing in a game and to become strongly motivated to commit themselves to the virtual world the game is creating with their help.

When students are learning a content area in school – such as some area of science – this domain could be seen as a special world of its own: the world of doing science in a certain way and acting with certain values. Students could be encouraged to take on identities as scientists of a certain sort, to see and think about themselves and their taken-for-granted everyday world in new ways. In this case, school would be functioning more like a good game than traditional schooling which stresses knowledge apart from action and identity.

RoN's tutorials: fish tanks

Let's begin to explore what makes *RoN* a good learning engine. When a player starts *RoN*, the designers immediately have two problems. First, learners are all different and the designers don't know what each one already knows, nor what their favored style of learning will be. Second, learners don't necessarily know themselves how much they do or do not already know and what their best style of learning will be in a given situation. Schools tend to handle these problems by assessing the learner and then deciding for the learner how these problems ought to be dealt with. *RoN*, like many other good games, solves the problem by letting learners assess themselves and learn things about what they do and do not know and what style of learning suits them here and now. Learners then decide for themselves how they want to proceed. Of course *RoN* is designed to assist learners in this task; they are not left solely to their own devices. By the time you have interacted with *RoN*'s tutorials and skill tests and played your first few real games, you know a good deal about yourself as a learner in general, and a learner of RTS games in particular. In this chapter the games called "Quick Battles" in *RoN* are what I refer to as the "real" game; a game called "Conquer the World" is also part of *RoN*, but I do not discuss that game here. Conquer the World is composed of Quick Battles and other elements.

When *RoN* starts, you see a screen with the following choices (the numbers on the right are dates, ranging from 60 AD to 1940):

		Tutorial	
Learn to Play	–	Quick Start	
Bodicia	–	Beginning Player	60
Alfred the Great	–	Beginning Player	878
The 100 Years War	–	Experienced Real-Time Strategy Player	1337
Henry VIII	–	Experienced Real-Time Strategy Player	1513
Battle of Britain	–	Advanced Topics	1940

Right away the learner sees choices: jump right in (Quick Start), learn step-by-step (moving from beginning player to experienced player to advanced topics), start with the experienced or advanced topics (thereby testing one's own assumptions about one's previous knowledge), or skip the tutorials altogether. Choice is built in from the beginning. Notice, too, there is no "remedial" in this learning world. You begin where you begin and move to advanced when you move there. None of this is timed. There are no invidious judgments based on one's previous "failures."

When the learner places the mouse on each choice above, a box is displayed at the bottom of the screen detailing just what historical event each choice will deal with and what skills the learner will learn by making that choice. Table 1 shows each choice and what is displayed in the box when the learner places the mouse over that choice.

All is not as it at first seems here though. What you see in the boxes are by no means all or even the majority of the skills you need to play *RoN* well. They are the "basic skills" you need to play the game, but "basic" in a special sense: they are the skills that allow you to actually start playing and learning from playing. I will point out below that the designers of *RoN* don't just take it for granted that players will be able to move from the basic skills in the tutorials to learning by playing. Once the players actually start the "real" game, they ensure that this transition – from basic skill learning to learning by playing – will happen. But before I tell you how they do this (it's all about players being able to customize the game to their own desires and goals), let me finish my discussion of the tutorials.

If we look back at the terms "experienced real-time strategy player" and "advanced topics" in Table 1 we see something interesting. "Experienced" and "advanced" mean something quite different here than they do in places like schools. The skills taught in the tutorials, as we have said, are "basic" (in the sense defined). They are not the deeper skills required to play *RoN* or any other RTS game well – skills like time management, speed, micromanaging many details at once, and strategic thinking. So it may seem odd that terms like "experienced" and "advanced" are used. But "experienced" and "advanced" here mean what players need to know to begin to take yet greater control over their own learning by discovery through playing. They don't mean "at the top of the vertical ladder

Table 1 Tutorial screens

Learn to Play – **Quick Start**		
Quick-learn learn-as-you-play introduction		
• One-on-one battle		
• Hints and suggestions as you play		
Bodicia – **Beginning Player**		60
Bodicia – Tutorial 2		
Help a queen fight off the Romans to reclaim her nation		
• Unit selection		
• Movement		
• Map scrolling		
• Help text		
• Basic combat		
Alfred the Great – **Beginning Player**		878
Alfred the Great – Tutorial 3		
Turn back the raging Viking horde		
• Constructing and using buildings		
• Training units		
• Minimap		
The 100 Years War – **Experienced Real-Time Strategy Player**		1337
The 100 Years War – Tutorial 4		
• Library research		
• Food, timber, and metal gathering		
• Capturing cities		
• Repairing buildings		
• Unit combat advantages and disadvantages		
• Transporting units across water		
Henry VIII – **Experienced Real-Time Strategy Player**		1513
Henry VIII – Tutorial 5		
Defend against Scottish raids		
• City construction		
• National borders		
• Knowledge and wealth gathering		
• Merchants and rare resources		
Battle of Britain – **Advanced Topics**		1940
Battle of Britain – Tutorial 6		
Battle the Germans in Britain's finest hour		
• Diplomacy		
• Air combat		
• Generals		
• Oil		
• Enhancement buildings		
• Formations		

of skills" (or "you get an A in this subject"). The player is experienced and advanced in the sense of being prepared for future learning "on site," not in the sense of necessarily being an expert.

Each tutorial places its basic skills in a scenario that is just a simplified version of the real game. This allows learners always to see how these basic skills fit into the game as a whole system and how different skills integrate with each other. In school, on the other hand, very often these days children are exposed to basic skills one by one, step by step. For example, in early reading instruction they are taught first awareness of the sounds that compose words, then the decoding of letters, then reading aloud to attain more fluent decoding, then comprehension skills (Coles 2003). Then and only then do they get to play the real "game" of reading, namely reading for meaning and to carry out their own purposes. In schools, too often, skills are decontextualized from the system (the "game") and from each other. This never happens in *RoN* or any other good game.

As an example of what I am trying to get at here, consider the tutorial labeled "Alfred the Great" (see Table 1). When you click on this tutorial, while the scenario is loading, you see the following in print, while listening to the same thing (my own remarks below are placed inside brackets):

> Eight hundred years after Bodicia rebelled against the Romans [this event was dealt with in the preceding tutorial labeled "Bodicia"], Britain was savaged by repeated Viking attacks. Alfred King of Wessex has been paying tribute to stave off the raiders, but in 878 the Vikings prepare for conquest. After a defeat, Alfred retreats to rebuild his forces and drive the Vikings away.

Once you press "Start" to start the scenario, you see the Vikings attacking the British town of Ethandum and hear the following: "Alfred suffers a stinging defeat when the Vikings attack in battle. The Norsemen loot the town and Alfred is driven back to his stronghold in Carlisle. Alfred must rebuild his forces and attempt to retake Ethandum."

Here we see that the scenario opens with a short context within which to understand and make sense of what one is going to do. After the Vikings' victory, the scene changes to the British town of Carlisle, the place to which Alfred has retreated. This is where we will play out our tutorial. We don't start from scratch though. We start in the Classical Age, the second of *RoN*'s eight ages, not in the Ancient Age where real games start. We also start with a large city, granary, lumber mill, market, and fort, as well as several citizens and their farms. While the game always starts with a (small) city and some citizens, the rest of these things players would normally build for themselves. Furthermore, while players in the real game always start with a library where they can do lots of different types of research, including research that leads to new ages, this scenario has no library, because we are not going to use it.

The setting of the scenario has been designed to be a minimal game setting with no more and no less than we need to learn at this point, but with enough to see how things fit together as a system. I will call this a "fish tank tutorial," because a fish tank can be, when done right, a simplified environment that lets one appreciate an ecosystem (e.g. a river, a pond, or reef in the ocean) by stripping away a good deal of complexity, but keeping enough to bring out some basic and important relationships.

As we stare at the town of Carlisle, we hear and see the following, which importantly gives us an overall purpose and goal within which to situate the actions we are going to carry out and the skills we are going to learn:

> The Vikings now control Ethandum. Before we can rally the nation, we must retake that city. Our first goal is to scout the Viking position and find a route for our attack. We need to keep watch on the Viking preparations and defenses. A Lookout [a type of building] is needed as close to the Vikings as possible. This is a good spot for the look out [the camera moves to a spot at the edge of the town and we see a big red circle marking the spot], close enough to see what's happening, but not so close that they'll notice it and attack. Now we'll learn how to construct new buildings. The action a selected citizen [the camera moves back to town and we see a big red circle marking a citizen] can perform is found in the lower left panel [we see a red arrow pointing to the panel]. Click the Build Military building button [we see a small yellow circle marking the button in the panel] to access a menu of building choices, one of which is the Lookout.

While you would normally have to click on the citizen to get the panel for types of buildings you can build (e.g. domestic ones, military ones, public monuments), in this case it is done for you when the game highlights the citizen. All you have to do is click on the Build Military Building button, which has a small flashing yellow circle around it. When you click on it, you see another panel appear – a panel for building different sorts of military buildings. This time there is a flashing yellow circle around the button for building a Lookout. We also hear "Select the highlighted Build Lookout button." Once we do this, we hear "Select the location for your Lookout by clicking near the target marker. Your citizen will begin construction there" and see a big red flashing circle at the spot that had been indicated earlier. When we click this spot, we hear "Good, now your citizen will move to that site and begin construction."

We are having our hands held as we move through the fish tank (it's what we can call a "supervised fish tank"). But notice some crucial features of this hand-holding. Information is given multimodally (Kress and van Leeuwen 2001): that is, in print, orally, and visually (note, as well, that if you place your mouse cursor on any person, building, or environmental object on the screen, a box will appear that tells you what it is and what you can do with it). There is lots of redundancy. Information is always given "just in time" when it can be used and we can see its meaning in terms of effects and actions. Unlike in school, we don't get lots of verbal information up front and then have to remember it all when we can actually use it much later.

We see clearly how each piece of information we are given and each skill we are learning (and doing) is interconnected to everything else we are learning and doing. We see the game as a system, not just a set of discrete skills. For example, we see how selecting a citizen, selecting a spot, and building a building are an integrated skill set. We see also how they relate to our overall purpose in this case: that is, to observe the enemy without getting too close. This lets us see that this skill set is both a general one (used for building and placing all sorts of buildings) and a *strategy* in the specific case when we are building Lookouts. In fact, we learn that all skills and skill sets are always ultimately strategies when they are concretely instantiated in practice.

This fish tank tutorial is also, of course, an example of what Vygotsky (1978) called learning within the learner's "Zone of Proximal Development." The "teacher" (in this case, the very design of the game) helps learners (players) pull off more than they could on their own and yet still feel a sense of personal accomplishment. Furthermore, the "teacher" (the design) tells the learner how to interpret things (what they mean), but these interpretations (meanings) become part and parcel of the learner's own mind as he or she carries out actions that embody those interpretations: e.g. building a Lookout as an initial plan in battle.

RoN's tutorials: supervised sandboxes

Each of the tutorials below "Quick Start" in Table 1 function as fish tanks. So, then, what about the Quick Start tutorial? By its placement at the top of the list you are coaxed to take this choice first, though you need not (and if you don't like it, you can always quit, go back to the main menu, and make another choice). If you click on Quick Start what you get, in fact, is something a bit different from a fish tank; you get what I call a "sandbox tutorial." In the real world, a sandbox is a piece of the real world, but sealed off to be a protected and safe place where children can explore. You can throw anything you want in the sandbox for the kids to play with so long as it isn't dangerous (there may be spiders in there, but presumably we don't let the family python in). It need not be as controlled and clean an environment as a fish tank.

So too the Quick Start tutorial is a space where the player is really playing the game, but is protected from quick defeat and is free to explore, try things, take risks, and make new discoveries. Nothing bad will happen. In other sorts of games, for example shooters, the first or first couple levels of the game often function as sandbox tutorials (e.g. the excellent *System Shock 2*), though they are not labeled as tutorials, but as real levels of the actual game (in the first level of *System Shock 2*, though it looks as if you must escape a failing spaceship rapidly and are in great danger, in actuality the level is not timed and the player cannot get hurt).

Quick Start starts by telling the player: "This is a preformed scenario where you can play the game at your own pace. Try to capture the Barbarian capital or conquer 70 percent of the map. There'll be hints and reminders to help you as you play."

The Quick Start scenario is actually the "real" game set at an easy level of difficulty with copious comments and hints. There is an opponent (in the real game you can have multiple opponents), but the opponent builds up slowly and does not make the smartest choices. The player gets a real sense of being in the game, even a sense of urgency, but can't really lose, or at least lose at all early before having put up a very good stand.

Let me show you just the beginning of the Quick Start tutorial, so that you get the flavor of what is going on. The material below deals with how I operated in the Quick Learn tutorial. Here once again I print my own remarks in brackets:

[Voice:] The leadership of your fledgling tribe has fallen on your shoulders. The first task is to unify a new nation under your rule. You're free to build your nation at your own pace. Occasionally you may receive advice to help keep things moving, but otherwise it's all up to you.

[If you wait, eventually you will read and hear hints about what to do. But there is "wait time" here to allow you to explore the screen and click on whatever you like. I clicked on the scout. When I did so I saw the box printed below and simultaneously heard the remarks listed below that:]

Scout: Currently selected (Hotkey)

Scouts, Ancient Age [picture with hotkey] – fast, but unarmed; good for exploring the map and finding enemies
Can spot hidden enemy units, such as spies and commandos
Can also destroy enemy spies
Strong vs. spies; Weak vs. Archers, Gunpowder Infantry

[Voice:] This is your scout. Use him to discover rare resources or locate the enemy position. Scouts are very fast and can see farther than most units, but cannot attack. You can move your scout around the map manually or click the auto explore button to have him explore on his own.

[After a few moments, I saw the message printed below on the top left of the screen and simultaneously heard the words below that:]

[Top Left Corner:] Create citizens to gather more resources

[Voice:] Your first priority in the Ancient Age is to create citizens and gather resources. Click your capital city and click Create Citizen to add to your work force. Put as many of your people to work gathering food and timber as you can. If you're running low on resources, you can always build farms to gather food and fill up woodcutter's camps with citizens to gather timber.

[During another "wait time," I clicked on the library and then clicked on a red button that lets the player research military technologies. Once this research is finished, the player can build military buildings. After clicking on the red button, I hear the following]:

[Voice:] Now that you have studied the first red military technology, you can build a barracks and begin training troops to protect your nation.

[After a few moments, I hear the following:]

[Voice:] If you want to see more of the map, you can always zoom in and out by using the mousewheel or pressing Page Up and Page Down on the keyboard.

The Quick Start tutorial goes on in this way for a while. If the player explores and does things, the tutorial confirms these acts and explains them. If the player waits, the tutorial prints a hint about what to do on the top left of the screen and says the hint orally and explains what it means. There are also, from time to time, remarks about how the game works: for example, the remark above about how to see more of the map. The tutorial is a nice dance of the player's actions and designers' guidance and instructions.

Midway through the Quick Start scenario the following box pops up:

MID GAME

At this point you should be having fun exploring the game and following some of the prompts that appear in the top left of the screen. If you're not having fun, you may want to try one of the following options.

I'm having fun I want to continue playing.
I need to know more basic information, take me back to the tutorial screen.
The game is too slow. Let me start a Quick Battle.

This box is an excellent example of alerting players to the fact that they need to assess their own progress, desires, and learning styles. They need to be proactive, make decisions, think about what they are doing and learning, and take control of their own learning.

When I started *RoN*, I started by doing the Quick Start tutorial. I did this for a rather perverse reason. I was so sure I would fail that I wanted to reconfirm my own view that actually playing the game would be too tedious and complex for me. What happened was that I got excited, feeling "Wow, I'm actually playing an RTS game and winning, to boot!" (of course, this may remind you of the great scene in the movie *What About Bob?* where the ever fearful Bob is lashed to the sail of a boat and yells to his friends, "Look, I'm sailing, I'm actually sailing!"). The Quick Start tutorial is a sandbox. The sandbox feels like the real world to a child, but is guaranteed not to destroy the child's trust and ego before he or she is strong enough to face more significant challenges. But this tutorial is a specific type of particularly efficacious sandbox. It is a sandbox with a wise parent present to guide and confirm efficacious play in the sandbox – in this case proactive game designers. Let's call this a "supervised sandbox."

Once I had done the Quick Start tutorial, I was energized to learn more, but of course I could not remember all the details the tutorial had introduced – nor was I meant to. Now I could turn to the specific fish tank tutorials and make each of these details, through focused practice, a part of my embodied intelligence and not just the caprice of my risky verbal memory. But I also knew now how these details fit into the larger scheme of the whole game, remembering that even in the fish tank tutorials skills are also introduced in terms of how they relate to other skills and to a simplified game system. Of course other learners might do the fish tank tutorials first and use the supervised sandbox of the Quick Start tutorial to assess their learning and readiness to jump into the "real" game.

There is one last important point to make about the Quick Start tutorial. What it does, in addition to what we have already surveyed, is introduce the *genre* of RTS games to players who may not have played such games before. "Genre" just means what *type* of thing something is: for example, whether a novel is a mystery, romance, science fiction, etc., or a piece of writing is a story, report, essay, and so forth. RTS games are one type of computer/video game (there are many others, e.g. shooters, adventure games, role-playing games). They involve typical actions, rules, and strategies that are different from those involved in other types of games.

Schools often try to teach kids to read and write, rather than read or write specific types of things like stories, reports, field notes, essays, or expositions. But, just like games, these different types of reading and writing operate by different principles and are used to carry out different types of actions. Good learning always involves knowing early and well what *type* of thing we are being asked to learn and do (Christe 1990; Cope and Kalantzis 1993; Martin 1990). Learners need to see this type of thing in action, not to be given static rules, if they are really to understand. In fact, for most types of things – like types of games, writing, movies, and so forth – there are no clear and static rules that define different types. Each type (e.g. an RTS game or an essay) is composed of many different instances that are variations around a theme. The only way to learn is to see some instances and live with them concretely.

Sure, there are some things you need to learn that help you to play most games regardless of their type (e.g. moving and clicking a mouse), but these are the tip of an iceberg compared to what you need to know about how different specific types of games work. Thinking an RTS game is a shooter will make you a particularly bad learner of the RTS game, or at the least will make you disappointed with it and not like it. The same thing is true of writing – there are some basic all-purpose things to learn (e.g. where to put commas and periods), but they too are but the tip of an iceberg, and writing an essay thinking it is supposed to be a personal narrative won't work.

RoN: unsupervised sandboxes

We are now ready – as the player is – to leave *RoN*'s tutorials and start the "real" game. I said that the skills *RoN*'s fish tank tutorials taught were "basic skills" in the sense that they are the skills that will allow you to actually start playing and learning from playing the game. The designers of *RoN* have ensured that these skills, once you learn them, will function just this way by building certain devices into the game play itself. When you leave the tutorials and actually start playing, there is a pause key that will stop time. This allows you to explore what icons on the screen mean and think about what you want to do. When time is paused, your opponent(s) do not continue building and so you do not have to worry about falling behind. Furthermore, you can set the game at one of two difficulty settings (easiest and easy) that greatly decreases the pressure of time. On these settings, opponents move slowly and not always in the smartest fashion. Finally, you can turn on (or off) hints that appear from time to time to remind you of what you have learned in the tutorials and teach you new things.

What all this means is that the player learns in the tutorial just enough to move on to learn more – and more subtle things – by actually playing the game, but playing it in a protected way so that deeper learning can occur through playing. The player can customize the game play to be, in fact, another sort of sandbox, in this case what we might call an unsupervised sandbox. The player is protected to explore and take risks, but aside from the small hint notes that can be turned off and on there is much less guidance and direction from *RoN*'s designers.

We see, then, that in *RoN* there is no clear division between the tutorials as a learning space and the player's first "real" games with difficulty set on easiest or easy and use of the pause key. These first real games are actually "hidden tutorials" which assist players in teaching themselves how to play *RoN*, not as a set of discrete skills, but as strategic thinking using an integrated system of skills. These unsupervised sandboxes make for a smooth transition between official tutorials and "really" playing the game (set on normal or a harder level).

Learning and playing

But there is a yet deeper principle at work here than the smooth transition between tutorials and playing. In a good game like *RoN* there is never a real distinction between learning and playing. The tutorials are simplified versions of playing the game. The game itself has a number of difficulty levels and at each level players must refine their skills and learn new ones. Players can also play other players in a multiplayer form of *RoN* on the Internet, getting into games with others whose skill levels are equivalent to their own. They can move up to play better and better players as their own skills progress, and, in doing so, will constantly be learning new things. When learning stops, fun stops, and playing eventually stops. For humans, real learning is always associated with pleasure and is ultimately a form of play – a principle almost always dismissed by schools.

There is one crucial learning principle that all good games incorporate that recognizes that people draw deep pleasure from learning and that such learning keeps people playing. Good games allow players to operate within, but at the outer edge of, their competence. At lots of moments, a good game feels highly challenging, but ultimately "doable." Perhaps the player fails a few times at a given task, but good games show how much progress the player has made on each try and the player sees that this progress is increasing each time he or she "fails." Eventually success comes. This feeling of the game being highly challenging, but ultimately doable, gives rise to a feeling of pleasurable frustration, one of the great joys of both deep learning and good gaming.

Good games, however, do not at all points operate at the outer and growing edge of the player's competence. This is because they also recognize another important learning principle: what I call the "principle of expertise," because it is the foundation of expertise in all significant domains (Bereiter and Scardamalia 1993). When learners learn a new skill set/strategy, they need to practice it over and over in varied contexts in order to make it operate at an almost unconscious routinized level. Then they are really good at it. But they are also in danger of resting on their laurels and learning nothing new. At this point, a good game throws a problem at the player where the routinized skill set/strategy won't work. This forces the player to think consciously again about skills that have become unconscious, taken-for-granted, and routine. The player must integrate his or her old skills with new ones, forming a new and higher skill set/strategy.

Now, in turn, the game will let this new skill set/strategy be practiced until it is routine. The player has moved to a new level of expertise and will then eventually face a yet harder problem that will start the process all over again. Thus good games cycle through times where they operate at the outer edge of (but within) the player's competence and times where they allow players to consolidate their skills. The times where players are consolidating their skills to the point of routine and taken-for-granted application give rise to another form of pleasure, the pleasure of mastery. Games cycle through periods of pleasurable frustration and routine mastery – a cycle of storm and calm.

These cycles are actually clearer in games like shooters (e.g. *Return to Castle Wolfenstein, Deus Ex, Unreal 2*) than they are in RTS games like *RoN*. In a game like *RoN* they are partially under the players' own control through the ways in which players can customize the game to their own skill level and interest. Players can themselves choose periods of skill consolidation and high challenge, though the game gives them plenty of feedback as to when things are getting too easy or too hard.

But how do players know when they are prepared to move beyond the unsupervised sandboxes they can create by playing the game on lower difficulty levels? How do they know when they are ready to move on to the more rigorous challenges of the normal difficulty level and harder levels, as well as multiplayer play? As it happens – as happened with me, in fact – the player can certainly tell the game is becoming too easy by how fast and thoroughly he or she gains victory over the opponent(s). However, I found that when I moved on to the normal level, it was at first too hard – harder than I had thought it would be, given my swift victories on lower difficulty levels. The problem of course was that I had not properly evaluated my skills. I did not realize that my skill sets/strategies were not fast and efficient enough to take on harder challenges.

RoN does two things to speak directly to this problem. First, it offers players a whole set of "Skill Tests." I list the skill tests in Table 2. Note that some tests are defined in terms of skills (e.g. mouse clicking) and others in terms of strategies (e.g. getting to the Classical Age fast). As we have said, in games skills are always seen as strategies.

These skill tests allow players to assess how well their skills fit into an efficient strategy set – how well integrated with each other and with the game as a system

Table 2 RoN skill tests

Skills Tests

1. Aging Madness – Age 2
How fast can you get to Classical Age? Find out if your resource management skill is good enough.

2. Aging Madness – Age 4
How fast can you get to Gunpowder Age? Find out if your resource management skill is good enough.

3. Aging Madness – Age 8
How fast can you get to the Information Age? Find out if your resource management skill is good enough.

4. Raiding Party
Take your bloodthirsty Mongol horde and pay a visit to some enemy towns in an exercise of micromanagement.

5. Hotkey Handling
Do you know your hotkeys? This is a test of hotkey knowledge.

6. Protect the Wonder
Protect your Wonder from jealous enemies in a exercise of defense.

7. Tactics
Defeat the enemy troops to take control of a valuable resource without losing more than half your army in this test of generalship.

8. Whack the General
How fast can you click your mouse? This is a test of clicking ability.

---

they are. The skill tests are, as they often are not in school, developmental for the learner and not evaluative (judgments carried out by authority figures). Furthermore, they are tests of what skills mean as strategies, not decontextualized tests of skills outside contexts of application where they mean quite specific things.

The second thing *RoN* does to solve the problem of letting players know where the cutting edge of their competence is is to render the whole matter *social*. Sadly, I failed my very first skill test several times. But I knew just how to increase my learning curve so I could pass the test. Every player knows there are an immense number of Internet sites and chat rooms from which loads of things can be learned and to which lots of questions can be directed.

One very effective thing – though there are a great many others – that players can do is download recordings of *RoN* games played by players at different levels of expertise. Players can watch these to learn new things at ever increasing levels of expertise. Players can also easily record their own games and review them. They can also pit the computer against itself – at whatever level of difficulty they choose – and watch how things are done. Online there is a worldwide university of peers and experts available to any player all the time. *RoN* lists its own website on its program file: a site with much information, chat rooms, and links to other sites. There are also published strategy guides and many games magazines that will discuss games like *RoN*, offering hints, guides, and other sorts of helpful information.

This social aspect of *RoN*, and games in general, makes *RoN* and other games the focus of what I have elsewhere called an "affinity group" (Gee 2003), and what I now prefer to call an "affinity space" (see Chapter 6) . An affinity space is a place or set of places where people can affiliate with others based primarily on shared activities, interests, and goals, not shared race, class, culture, ethnicity, or gender. They have an affinity for a common interest or endeavor (like *RoN*). The many websites and publications devoted to *RoN* create a social space in which people can, to any decree they wish, small or large, affiliate with others to share knowledge and gain knowledge that is distributed and dispersed across many different people, places, Internet sites, and modalities (e.g. magazines, chat rooms, guides, recordings). Distributed and dispersed knowledge that is available "just in time" and "on demand" is, then, yet another learning principle built into a game like *RoN*. Too often in schools knowledge is not shared across the students, is not distributed so that different students, adults, and technologies offer different bits and pieces of it as needed, and is not garnered from dispersed sites outside the classroom (for a case where it was, see Brown 1994). *RoN* has no such problems.

Conclusion

By way of summary, let me collect together here in a list some of the learning principles that are built into *RoN* and reflected in my interaction with the game. I believe that these principles would be efficacious in areas outside games: for example, in science instruction in schools, though I must leave that argument for another time. However, it is clear that these principles resonant with what theorists in the learning sciences have said about learning in content areas in school.

1 They create motivation for an extended engagement.
2 They create and honor preparation for future learning.
3 They create and honor horizontal learning experiences, not just vertical ones.
4 "At risk" doesn't need to mean any more than that you don't need another bad learning experience.
5 They let learners themselves assess their previous knowledge and learning styles and make decisions for themselves (with help).
6 They build in choice from the beginning.
7 They banish "remedial" – the word and the experience.
8 "Basic skills" means what you need to learn in order to start taking more control over your own learning and learn by playing.
9 "Experienced" doesn't need to mean "expert"; it can mean that one is well prepared for future learning.
10 They teach basic skills in the context of simplified versions of the real game so that learners can see how these skills fit into the game as a system and how they integrate with each other.
11 They teach skills as sets and make it clear how they are instantiated in practice as strategies for accomplishing specific goals or carrying out specific activities.
12 They offer supervised (i.e. guided) fish tank tutorials (simplified versions of the real system).
13 They offer supervised (i.e. guided) sandbox tutorials (safe versions of the real system).
14 They give information via several different modes (e.g. in print, orally, visually). They create redundancy.
15 They give information "just in time" and "on demand."
16 Learning should be a collaborative dance between the teacher's (designer's) guidance and the learner's actions and interpretations.
17 They let learners create their own unsupervised sandboxes (i.e. let them be able to customize what you are offering).
18 They teach learners the genre they are involved with early and well (supervised sandboxes are good for this).
19 They ensure that there is a smooth transition between tutorials and actually playing (customized unsupervised sandboxes are good for this).
20 There should be no big distinction between learning and playing at any level.
21 They allow learners to discover the outer edge of their competence and to be able to operate just inside that edge.
22 They allow learners to practice enough so that they routinize their skills and then challenge them with new problems that force them to re-think these taken-for-granted skills and integrate them with new ones. Repeat.

23 They offer learners developmental (not evaluative) skill tests that allow them to judge where the outer edge of their competence is and that let them make decisions about what new things they need to learn on their path to mastery.

24 They ensure that learners at every level of expertise can readily use knowledge that is distributed and dispersed across a great many other people, places, sites, texts, tools, and technologies.

25 They ensure that the learners have and use an affinity space wherein they can interact with peers and masters, near and far, around a shared interest (even passion), making use of distributed and dispersed knowledge.

Young people exposed to these principles so powerfully in a game like *RoN* are engaged in a form of learning that, in my view, makes many schools look uninspired and out of touch with the realities of how human learning works at a deep level. Perhaps, too, this exposure causes in some of these young people a critique of schooling as it currently exists.

6

AFFINITY SPACES

Introduction: from groups to spaces

I have argued throughout this book that people learn best when their learning is part of a highly motivated engagement with social practices which they value. A wide body of research, applied to schools and workplaces, has pointed to the importance of "communities of practice" in this process (Lave 1996; Lave and Wenger 1991; Rogoff 1990; Wenger 1998). In this research, learning is looked at in terms of apprenticeship. Learners "apprentice" themselves to a group of people who share a certain set of practices (e.g. learning to cook in a family, learning to play video games with a guild, learning to assemble circuit boards in a workplace, learning to splice genes in a biology lab), pick up these practices through joint action with more advanced peers, and advance their abilities to engage and work with others in carrying out such practices.

There is no doubt that communities of practice are an important force in learning in the modern world. However, in this chapter, I want to consider another important social configuration in which people participate and learn. I will focus on the idea of a *space* in which people interact, rather than on membership in a community.

The notion of a "community of practice" has been a fruitful one and there are certainly many cases where the term is apt (see Wenger *et al.* 2002 for a clear demarcation of what is and what is not a community of practice). However, it has given rise to several problems, some of which are:

1 The idea of "community" can carry connotations of "belongingness" and close-knit personal ties among people which do not necessarily always fit classrooms, workplaces, or other sites where the notion of a community of practice has been used.
2 The idea of "community" seems to bring with it the notion of people being "members." However, "membership" means such different things across different sorts of communities of practice and there are so many different ways and degrees of being a member in some communities of practice that it is not clear that membership is a truly helpful notion.
3 While Wenger (see Wenger *et al.* 2002) has tried to be careful in delineating

77

just what is and what is not a community of practice, distinguishing it from other sorts of affiliations, the notion has been used by others to cover such a wide array of social forms that we may be missing the trees for the forest.

In my view, the key problem with notions like "community of practice" is that they make it look like we are attempting to label a group of people. Once this is done, we face vexatious issues over which people are in and which are out of the group, how far they are in or out, and when they are in or out. The answers to these questions vary (even their very answerability varies) greatly across different social groupings. If we start with the notion of a "community" we can't go any further until we have defined who is in and who is not, since otherwise we can't identify the community. Yet it is often issues of participation, membership, and boundaries that are problematic in the first place.

Take a high-school science class. Johnny and Janie are both in the class. Janie is proactively attempting to engage with the science in the class, but Johnny is "playing the game" for a passing grade. Are they in the same community of practice or is Janie in a school science community of practice and Johnny in a "doing school" community of practice? What sense does it make to say all the students in this class are in some (one?) community of practice just because they are all contained by the same four walls? Or if we think beyond those four walls, if some parents are helping their children in science, are they in the community of practice too? What about the principal, the other science teachers, the reading specialist who comes into the class once a week, the author of the textbook, or for that matter the curriculum specialists and policy-makers who help shape the classroom's practices in regard to science and schooling more generally?

I suggest that the problem here is trying to start with a label (like community of practice) which looks like a label for a group of people, a group which must then be identified in terms of its "members." What I want to suggest instead is that (at least sometimes) we start with "spaces" and not groups.

Let me start with an analogy. It is hard to say who is and who is not an "American." (I mean by this not who is officially a "citizen," but who adopts "American culture," whatever that may mean. There are people who are not citizens who impress me as very "American" and there are citizens who impress me as not very "American.") For some purposes, it may be easier to draw the boundaries of the United States as a geographical space on a map and then look at how different sorts of people use that space: i.e. what they do there and what they get from that space (e.g. import or export from it). In the case of Johnny and Janie in the science class, the two students are taking quite different things from the space.

If we start by talking about spaces rather than "communities," we can then go on and ask to what extent the people interacting within a space, or some subgroup of them, do or do not actually form a community. The answer will be different in different cases. Even if the people interacting within a space do not constitute a community in any real sense, they still may get a good deal from their interactions with others and share a good deal with them. Indeed, some people interacting within a space may see themselves as sharing a "community" with others in that space, while other people view their interactions in the space differently. In any case, creating spaces wherein diverse sorts of people can interact is a leitmotif of the modern world.

I don't want to talk just about physical or geographical spaces. Just as people can enter a physical space like the United States, they can enter a virtual space like a website or a chat room. People interacting with each other about a specific disease on a patient empowerment website are in a virtual space together. There are spaces that are mixtures of the real and the virtual, such as a meeting in which some people are physically together in a room and others are interacting with the group via the Internet or over a video conferencing system. People who play chess with each other by sending moves via email or letter are interacting, at a distance, in a space created by email or the postal service. Modern technologies allow the creation of more and more spaces where people can enter and interact with others (and with objects and tools) at a distance. So when I talk about "spaces" I don't mean just physical spaces.

My goal, however, is not just or primarily to introduce this idea of spaces. Rather it is to discuss a particular type of space, which I will call an "affinity space." I will first define what I mean by a space generally and then define what I mean by an affinity space in particular. When I get to affinity spaces, I will argue that they capture one characteristically modern and important form of social affiliation – one that can fruitfully be compared and contrasted with other forms (Gee 2000–1). I will define what I mean by a space through one concrete example – an example that also happens to be an affinity space. This will allow me to characterize what makes this example a space and then turn to what makes it an affinity space.

Semiotic social spaces: *AoM*

To define what I mean by a space, I will use "real-time strategy" (RTS) computer games as the basis for an illustrative example, using the game *Age of Mythology* ("*AoM*" for short) as a paradigmatic instance of such a game (see http://www. microsoft.com/games/ageofmythology/greek_home.asp). In a RTS game (like the game *RoN* we discussed in the last chapter), the player builds buildings, settlements, towns, and/or cities for a given "civilization," using workers to collect gold, farm land, cut wood, and hunt animals to gain the necessary resources for building and sustaining his or her civilization. As the player builds various types of buildings, he or she can use the buildings to construct or train different types of warriors and military apparatus, as well as other types of actors such as priests or scientists (e.g. in *AoM* one can use a Temple to gain mythological figures, an Academy to train Hoplites, an Archery Range to train archers, a Stable to train cavalry, a Fortress to train heroes, a Dock to build various types of boats, a Town Center to get more villagers, etc., through many other choices).

Eventually, the player goes off with his or her "army" to fight one or more other players (real people or the computer) who have also been building up their civilizations during the same time. If the player waits too long, the opponent may be too strong; if the player does not take enough time to build up properly, he or she may be too weak to fight well. Timing is important and so are the decisions about what and where to build (and there are always a great many options).

In *AoM* the "civilizations" one can play are ancient Greeks, Romans, or Norse, building buildings from these ancient civilizations and eventually gaining, for example, various types of Greek soldiers, heroes, military apparatus, and mythological figures to fight other civilizations. On the other hand, in *Galactic Battlegrounds* (a *Star Wars* game), the "civilizations" one can play are the Trade Federation, Gungans, Royal Naboo, Rebel Alliance, Galactic Empire, or Wookies – all groups from the *Star Wars* universe. In *Galactic Battlegrounds*, the buildings, soldiers, heroes and apparatus are all specific to one of these groups. For each "civilization" in this game there are over 160 choices about what to build or train – each choice having consequences for the other choices one makes. This is typical of the level of complexity in RTS games.

Now I will define a space step by step. To define any space, we need first to start with some *content* – something for the space to be "about." Whatever gives the space some content, I will call a *generator*. In the case of RTS games, one of the generators of the content is, of course, an actual game like *AoM*. Such games offer up a characteristic set of multimodal signs (words, images, graphs, etc.) to which people can give specific sorts of meanings and with which they can interact in various ways. We have seen some of these above: "civilizations," warriors and heroes, buildings, and real-time competition. In a cooking club, the cookbooks and shared recipes are generators.

Once we have one or more generators, we have some content – something for the space to be "about." Given this content, we can look at the space in two different ways. First, we can look at it directly in terms of *content*, i.e. what signs it has and how they are organized. Second, we can look at it in terms of how people *interact* with that content or with each other over that content.

The same distinction can be made for a painting. We can view a painting as content: that is, as a work of art designed in a certain way. Notice that content always brings up the issue of design, since someone has to design the content. Or we can view the painting in terms of how people react to, use, or interact with the painting and with each other over the painting. To say of a Monet painting that "It is made up of a myriad of pastel dabs" or "It depicts a hayfield in the early morning light" is to comment on its content (and the design of that content). To say that the painting "Makes people feel they are present in the field" or that "Most people appreciate the painting best when they stand at a fair distance from it" or that "People strongly disagree in terms of how realistic they think the painting is" is to comment on how people interact with the painting or with each other over the painting.

We have already seen above some of the content in *AoM* and other RTS games. If we point out that in such games there are trees, farms, and gold that can be collected and used as resources with which to build buildings, we are talking about the content of the space. Indeed, this is just part of the basic content of all RTS games.

On the other hand, people actually play RTS games in the world. Different players use different strategies. People sometimes play such games alone and sometimes with other people on the Internet. They may also talk to other players about such games and read magazines and Internet sites devoted to them. When we talk about how people play such games and how they organize their own behaviors and their interactions with other people in regard to RTS games, we are talking about the space in interactional terms.

To take a content view of the space of RTS games is to ask about the design of such games. To take an interactional view of the space of RTS games is to ask about the ways in which people organize their thoughts, beliefs, values, actions, and social interactions in relation to the signs made available in such games.

What is wonderful about computer and video games is that people can interact so directly with the content of the game. In a RTS game, a virtual "citizen" goes out and farms or collects wood. But the human player manipulates the virtual citizen – i.e. moves him or her to the farm or the forest. Here content and inter-action come directly together, because the virtual character is part of the content of the game, but the manipulation of the character is an interaction made by the human player. Of course interaction goes much further than this, since people can interact with the game and each other in regard to the game in a myriad of different ways.

Let us say, then, that every space has a "content organization" (that is, how its content is designed or organized) and an "interactional organization" (namely, how people organize their thoughts, beliefs, values, actions, and social interactions in regard to those signs and their relationships). The content organization of a game emerges from the work of designers. The interactional organization emerges from people's actions and interactions with and over the space (in this case, *AoM*) as these begin to take on some (however loose) regularity or patterning.

And of course the actions of people helping to form the interactional organi-zation of the space as a set of social practices and typical identities can rebound on the actions of those helping to design the content of the space, since the designers must react to the pleasures and displeasures of the people interacting with the content they have designed. At the same time, the actions of those designing the content rebound on the actions of those helping to organize the interaction organi-zation as a set of social practices and identities, since that content shapes and transforms (though by no means fully determines) those practices and identities.

But one more thing is needed to define a space: namely, one or more *portals* that people can use to enter the space (remember, it's a type of space, not a group of people). A portal is anything that gives access to the content and to ways of interacting with that content, by oneself or with other people.

For *AoM*, there are a number of different portals. The disk on which the game comes, slipped into a computer so that one can play the game by oneself, is one such portal. An Internet site on which a player can play the game against other players is another portal. An Internet site in which players discuss the game or download content about the game is another portal. The strategy guide for *AoM*, which one can purchase (a book replete with information about the game, recommended strategies, and a complete walkthrough of the single-player campaign), is also a portal. Each of these portals gives one access to the signs (content) used in *AoM*. There are many others.

Portals are places where people get access to interact with the content generators generate. But portals can also be or become generators themselves (though this is not always the case), if they allow people to add to content or change the content other generators have generated. So, for example, it is common on game sites on the Internet for fans to offer others new maps on which to play the game or to allow others to access recordings of games they have played to learn how to play better. In this case, the portal is also a generator, since people (who are not the game's designers) are making new content for others.

Likewise, a generator can also be a portal, though this need not always be the case (think of a teacher's manual that students never see; it is a generator but not a portal for the students, though it is a portal for the teacher). As we have said, the game disk is both a generator (it offers up the signs or content) and a portal, since one can use it to play the game and thereby interact with the signs.

Let us pause a moment to ask how these terms would apply to a science classroom and what sorts of questions they would lead us to ask. We first have to ask what the generator is that is the (or a) source of the sign system (content) that the classroom is interacting with. In the classroom this might be the textbook, the teacher, lab materials, and/or other things. For analytical purposes, we could restrict ourselves to one generator or consider several at a time. We also might (or might not) find that the textbook functions as the core or original generator.

We can then ask questions about how the signs generated by the generator are designed to communicate a certain content. This is to ask about the content organization of the space. In turn, we can ask questions about what sorts of thoughts, values, deeds, interactions, and identities people take up in regard to these signs. This is to ask about the interactional organization of the space.

We can also ask questions about how the content and interactional organizations reflexively shape each other, if indeed they do: i.e. how does the content (and its design) shape thought, deed, and practice and how do thought, deed, and practice shape and re-shape (re-design) content? (For example, does the teacher rethink the content based on student beliefs, actions, and interactions? Do new editions of the textbook change, based on changing beliefs, values, and practices? Do new generators or revisions of old ones change people's thoughts, deeds, and interactions?)

We can also ask about portals: that is, what gives students access to interactions with the signs, either by themselves or with others. The generator is often a portal (e.g. the textbook), but there are other portals as well. For example, one portal may be small group discussions, another might be question-and-answer sessions

82

between the teacher and the class, another might be lab work. Of course we would want to know who uses each portal and how, as well as the ways in which the portal shapes thought and interaction.

Finally, we can ask whether a generator is also a portal. Of course if the students have a textbook and use it, this generator is also a portal. However, if the teacher is following a teacher's manual that the students never see, this is a generator that is not in fact a portal for the students (though it is for the teacher). And we can also ask if portals ever become generators themselves. For example, can students through, say, their group work on a project change the sign system (content) with which the class is interacting in any serious way? Can they add new signs, subtract signs, or change the relationship among the signs that the class is interacting with? If so, the portal of the group project is also a generator; otherwise it is not.

Let me hasten to add that it is degrees that are often of most importance here, not simply binary distinctions. We really want to know, for instance, how strong a generator a given portal is, not just whether it is one or not (perhaps it is a very weak one). We want to know whether content organization and interactional organization reflexively shape each other in strong or weak ways, not just whether they do or not.

Affinity spaces

I want now to turn to a particular type of space that I will call an "affinity space." Affinity spaces are a particularly common and important form today in our high-tech new capitalist world. It is instructive to compare affinity spaces to the sorts of spaces that are typical in schools, which usually do not have the features of affinity spaces. This comparison is particularly important because many young people today have lots of experience with affinity spaces, and thus have the opportunity to compare and contrast their experiences with these to their experiences in classrooms.

Let's return to *Age of Mythology*. The core generator for *AoM* as a space (remember this is a subspace of the larger RTS game space) is of course the game itself. Its content organization is typical of RTS games: a form that has been shaped quite strongly by the demands, pleasures, and displeasures of players. This is true not only over time, as RTS games change in response to player reactions, but also in the present. Games like *AoM* offer players (sometimes repeated) "patches" over the Internet to correct problems of many sorts players have discovered. Thus this core generator is continually updated; the content organization is continually transformed by the interactional organization of the space.

The portals to *AoM* as a space are, of course, the game (single-player and multiplayer), but also strategy guides, official websites and fan websites. These portals, as we will see below, are also all fairly strong generators, adding to and changing the relationships among the signs generated by the *AoM* core generator (i.e. the game).

To define *AoM* as not just a space, but also an affinity space, I want to look at just one of its portals, namely the website *AoM* Heaven (http://AoM.heaven games.com), a fan-produced website. It would take several hundred pages to print this site out (not counting its many links to other sites) and it is updated every day. Some of the many things one can access from this site are:

- the latest news about *AoM*, the company that made the game, what players are doing, and when and where they can play games against each other;
- polls that take votes on various questions and issues (e.g. "Have you played any custom scenarios for *AoM*?"; "What do you think is the most useful classical age myth unit?"; or "What aspect of the Norse culture impresses you most?");
- previews and reviews of *AoM* and other RTS games;
- interviews with people about *AoM* and related matters;
- forums (discussion groups) to which one can contribute, each devoted to a different topic germane to *AoM*, including general discussions, strategy, the new expansion pack, technical issues, scenario design, mythology, clan discussions (a clan is a group that plays together), and other topics;
- links to other sites of interest to people interested in *AoM* or other RTS games;
- ladder forums that give the rankings and scores of players who play against others on the Internet;
- FAQs (frequently asked questions) that explain various aspects of the game and give players help with the game;
- strategy guides and walkthroughs for "newbies" (new players);
- general information about and pictures of a new expansion of *AoM* that will appear soon (*Titians X-Pack*);
- game information which gives technical details and statistics about all aspects of the game (e.g. how long it takes to build each type of building);
- images from the game and artwork, including art by fans, inspired by the game;
- downloads of many different sorts, including new maps and scenarios made by players, recorded instances of multiplayer games, and even improvements players have made to different parts of the game's "AI" (artificial intelligence): for example, improvements to the "AI" used on maps with a lot of water or even programs players can use to adjust the AI in different ways each time they play the game.

This portal to the *AoM* space has a set of features that are definitive of what I will call an "affinity space." I describe each of these features below. Together they constitute a definition of an affinity space. Let me make it clear here though that what people have an affinity with (or for) in an affinity space is not first and foremost the other people using the space, but the endeavor or interest around which the space is organized, in this case the RTS game *AoM*. We do not have to see an affinity space as an all-or-nothing thing. Rather we can say that any space that has more of these features than another is more of an affinity space than the other or is closer to being a paradigmatic affinity space. The features defining an affinity space (eleven in all) – as these are exemplified by *AoM* – are as follows:

1 **Common endeavor, not race, class, gender, or disability, is primary**

In an affinity space, people relate to each other primarily in terms of common interests, endeavors, goals, or practices, not primarily in terms of race, gender, age, disability, or social class. These latter variables are backgrounded, though they can be used (or not) strategically by people if and when they choose to use them for their own purposes. This feature is particularly enabled and enhanced in *AoM* Heaven because people enter this and other *AOM* portals with an identity (and name) of their own choosing. They can make up any name they like and give any information (fictional or not) about themselves they wish to. This identity need not – and usually does not – foreground the person's race, gender, age, disability, or social class.

2 **Newbies and masters and everyone else share common space**

This portal does not segregate newcomers ("newbies") from masters. The whole continuum of people from new to experienced, from unskilled to highly skilled, from minorly interested to addicted, and everything in between, is accommodated in the same space. They each can get different things out of the space – based on their own choices, purposes, and identities – and still mingle with others as they wish, learning from them when and where they choose (even "lurking" on advanced forums where they may be too unskilled to do anything but listen in on the experts). Affinity spaces may have portals where people with more expertise are segregated from people with less (e.g. players usually choose whom they will play against on multi-player game sites in terms of their level of expertise), but they also have ones where such segregation does not occur.

3 **Some portals are strong generators**

The portal allows people to generate new signs and relationships among signs for the *AoM* space. That is, the portal is also a major generator. Fans create new maps, new scenarios for the single-player and multiplayer games, adjust or redesign the technical aspects of the game, create new artwork, and even give tutorials on mythology as it exists in the game or outside the game world.

4 **Content organization is transformed by interactional organization**

Based on what the players do and say on sites like *AoM* Heaven, the core original generator (the game) is changed via patches, new content, and new expansions offered by the company that makes the game. That is, the content of *AoM* as a space is transformed by the actions and interactions of players acting and interacting on sites like *AoM* Heaven.

5 **Both intensive and extensive knowledge are encouraged**

The portal encourages and enables people who use it to gain and spread both intensive knowledge and extensive knowledge. They can readily develop and display specialized knowledge (intensive knowledge), in one or more areas: for example, learning how to tweak the game's AI and advising others in this area. At the same time, the portal encourages and enables people to gain a good deal of broader, less specialized, knowledge about many aspects of the space (extensive knowledge), which they share with a great many others who use the portal or otherwise use the *AOM* space. Intensive knowledge is specialized, extensive knowledge is less specialized, broader, and more widely shared. This creates people who share lots of knowledge, but each have something special to offer.

6   **Both individual and distributed knowledge are encouraged**
      The portal also encourages and enables people both to gain individual knowledge (stored in their heads) and to learn to use and contribute to distributed knowledge. Distributed knowledge is knowledge that exists in other people, material on the site (or links to other sites), or in mediating devices (various tools, artifacts, and technologies) and to which people can connect or "network" their own individual knowledge. Such knowledge allows people to know and do more than they could on their own. People are encouraged and enabled to act with others and with various mediating devices (e.g. level editors, routines for tweaking the AI of the game, strategy guides) in such a way that their partial knowledge and skills become part of a bigger and smarter network of people, information, and mediating devices.

7   **Dispersed knowledge is encouraged**
      The portal also encourages and enables people to use dispersed knowledge: that is, knowledge that is not actually at the site itself, but at other sites or in other spaces. For example, the portal enables and encourages people to learn about mythology in general, including mythological facts and systems that go well beyond *AoM* as a game. Much of this information is not directly in the *AoM* Heaven site, but on other sites it links to or in books or movies the site will mention or review. When a space utilizes dispersed knowledge it means that its distributed knowledge exists in a quite wide and extensive network. When knowledge is dispersed in a space, the space does not set strict boundaries around the areas from which people will draw knowledge and skills.

8   **Tacit knowledge is encouraged and honored**
      The portal encourages, enables, and honors tacit knowledge – that is, knowledge players have built up in practice, but may not be able to explicate fully in words. This knowledge may be about how to play the game, how to design new maps and scenarios for the game, how to form a forum party, or a great many other things. Players pass on this tacit knowledge via joint action when they interact with others via playing the game with them or interacting with them in other spaces. At the same time, the portal offers ample opportunities for people, if they wish, to try to (learn to) articulate their tacit knowledge in words, for example when they contribute to a forum on technical matters like how to design good maps.

9   **There are many different forms and routes to participation**
     People can participate in *AoM* Heaven or other portals to the *AoM* space in
     many different ways and at many different levels. People can participate
     peripherally in some respects, centrally in others; patterns can change from
     day to day or across longer stretches of time.

10   **There are lots of different routes to status**
     A portal like *AoM* Heaven, and the *AoM* space as a whole, allows people to
     achieve status if they want it (and they may not) in many different ways.
     Different people can be good at different things or gain repute in a number of
     different ways. Of course playing the game well can gain one status, but so
     can organizing forum parties, putting out guides, working to stop hackers
     from cheating in the multiplayer game, posting to any of a number of differ-
     ent forums, or a great many other things.

11   **Leadership is porous and leaders are resources**
     A space like *AoM* and a portal to it like *AoM* Heaven do not have "bosses."
     They do have various sorts of leaders – people who design the game or the
     website – though we have seen that the boundary between leader and
     follower is vague and porous, since players can generate content for the game
     or site. Leadership in a affinity space like *AoM* consists of designers,
     resourcers (i.e. they resource other people), and enablers (teachers). They
     don't and can't order people around or create rigid, unchanging, and
     impregnable hierarchies.

Affinity spaces are common today in our global high-tech new capitalist world
(Gee 2000–1; Rifkin 2000). Many businesses organize such spaces for their
customers. For example, the company that makes the Saturn car creates websites
and activities (e.g. social gatherings, newsletters, Internet chat rooms) around
which its customers can identify as Saturn owners. Businesses in the new capitalist
era (Gee *et al.* 1996) of cross-functional, dispersed, networked teams and project-
based work often seek to create affinity spaces to motivate, organize, and resource
their "partners" (they seek to avoid the term "worker" which implies a traditional
boss–worker relationship in which one party "bosses" the other).

Social activists, whether their cause be ecology, anti-globalization, or school
vouchers, also often organize themselves and others in terms of affinity spaces
(Beck 1999). In such spaces, people who may share little and even differ dramatic-
ally on other issues, affiliate around their common cause and the practices
associated with espousing it via affinity spaces that have most or all of the above
eleven features. Fans of everything (e.g. movies, comic books, television shows,
video games, various lifestyle choices) create and sustain affinity spaces of which
AoM is of course just one of a great many. Scientists in many different disciplines
network with colleagues, funders, policy-makers, and the public across the globe
via networks of activities, newsletters and other sorts of texts, websites, computer
bulletin boards, email chains, and conferences in ways that have progressively
taken on more and more of the features of an affinity space.

There have of course been educators who have sought to create in classrooms something akin to an affinity space. The best-known efforts here perhaps were Ann Brown and Joseph Campione's classroom "learning communities" (see Brown 1994 for an overview). In my view, these "communities" – at least as they were described in idealized ways – could better be viewed as affinity spaces than as communities in any traditional sense. They involved the use of multiple sorts of mediating devices (computers and email to outside experts), distributed knowledge as students worked in teams with those mediating devices, dispersed knowledge as students drew on expertise outside the classroom, intensive knowledge as individual students chose to "major" in some aspect of the curriculum and help other students in that respect, and extensive shared knowledge as the students taught each other different parts of a common curriculum (via the jigsaw method, Aronson 1978).

Since at times the students taught each other, they took over some of the teacher's traditional leadership role. These classrooms incorporated a number of the remaining eleven features above as well, and one could imagine this process (largely stopped today by our return to "the basics" and skill-and-drill under the new accountability and testing agenda) going much further (to the point where not all students would actually be in the classroom together face to face each day).

However, if we compare the eleven features of an affinity group to most classrooms today, we usually find that the classroom either does not have a given feature or has it much more weakly than a prototypical affinity space. In classrooms the common endeavor (that which they are supposed to have affinity with) is often unclear (e.g. "science," "doing school," "school-science") to the students, and race, class, gender, and disability are often much more foregrounded than they are in an affinity space. Furthermore, race, class, gender, and disability are often much less flexible in classrooms and serve much less as resources students can use strategically for their own purposes.

In classrooms students are segregated by things like grade level, ability, and skills more often than they are mixed together across the whole continuum of these. Even in heterogeneous groupings the differences are small compared to the differences one can find and access in an affinity space. For example, I myself am light years away from being able to understand how to program anything that would modify the AI of a computer game, yet I can access such information and the people connected to it at *AoM* Heaven (and did so and actually learned a lot).

In classrooms portals are rarely strong generators where students both interact with the signs that constitute the content of the classroom instruction and are able to modify, transform, and add to them as well. Furthermore, rarely is the core generator (e.g. the textbook or the curriculum guide) modified ("patched") in an ongoing way based on student desires, pleasures, displeasures, actions, and interactions.

In classrooms students are encouraged to gain pretty much the same knowledge across the board – knowledge which is often extensive and not intensive – or some students are encouraged and enabled to gain intensive knowledge, but others are not. Furthermore, when some students do gain intensive knowledge, they are rarely allowed to teach the teacher and the other students. In an affinity space no one is stopped from gaining intensive knowledge because someone else thinks they are "my low students" or "struggling." Classrooms are rarely spaces where everyone shares lots of interests and knowledge (extensive knowledge), while each person has his or her own intensive knowledge to add as a potential resource for others.

Classrooms tend to encourage and reward individual knowledge stored in the head, not distributed knowledge. They don't often allow students to network with each other and with various tools and technologies and be rewarded for doing so, rather than being rewarded for individual achievement. Furthermore, classrooms tend to narrowly constrain where students can gain knowledge, rather than utilize widely dispersed knowledge. Furthermore, they rarely honor, or even acknowledge for that matter, tacit knowledge that cannot (at least for now) be verbally articulated. In turn, they usually do a poor job in giving students help and practice with learning how to articulate such tacit knowledge, when and where it can be articulated (and it cannot always be articulated).

Classrooms usually do not have multiple routes to participation, engaging their students in different ways, to different levels, in different contexts. They usually do not have multiple routes to status; rather, students get As for narrow reasons, the same for all. Finally, in classrooms leadership is not usually porous, where it is at times hard to tell who is leading and who is following, where students sometimes lead and teachers follow, and where leadership is constituted by resourcing others and designing environments where they can learn on their own terms, rather than dictating what people "need" to do, believe, say, and write.

But, one may ask: "So what? What does it matter that schools don't use affinity spaces? Why should they?" At this point I can only state a hypothesis in answer to these questions. Young people today are confronted with and enter more and more affinity spaces. They see a different and arguably powerful vision of learning, affiliation, and identity when they do so. Learning becomes both a personal and a unique trajectory through a complex space of opportunities (i.e. a person's own unique movement through various affinity spaces over time) and a social journey as one shares aspects of that trajectory with others (who may be very different from oneself and inhabit otherwise quite different spaces) for a shorter or longer time before moving on. What these young people see in school may pale by comparison. It may seem to lack the imagination that infuses the non-school aspects of their lives (Gee 2003). At the very least they may demand an argument for "Why school?"

7

SHAPE-SHIFTING
PORTFOLIO PEOPLE

Old literacies

Sociocultural studies of literacy (Barton 1994; Gee 1996; Street 1995) – sometimes called "The New Literacy Studies" – have argued that "literacy" is not one thing. Rather, there are as many different "literacies" as there are socioculturally distinctive practices into which written language is incorporated. For example, the sorts of writing and reading that people do on a fan fiction site – let's say one devoted to Sailor Moon – constitute a distinctive "literacy." However, one family of literacy practices has served for some time now as the most significant gate to economic success and sociopolitical power in our society. These are reading and writing practices that incorporate "academic language."

Academic language does not exist just in schools; it exists, as well, out in the world of disciplinary, professional, bureaucratic, official, and public-sphere practices and institutions (Schleppegrel 2004; Schleppegrel and Cecilia Colombi 2002). As we saw earlier, in Chapters 2 and 3, academic language is itself not one thing, but is composed of a family of related varieties. Furthermore, each of these varieties has spoken forms as well as written ones.

However significant it is, academic language is but one family of specialist language varieties. We saw earlier that people, even quite young ones, learn specialist varieties of language when they learn the Pokémon universe or become video gamers. Academic language is acquired in school, though it is facilitated at home by families with a good deal of mainstream educational and cultural capital. It comes to form for some learners (provided they give it allegiance and identify with it) a specific type of "consciousness" or "worldview": what the Scollons once called "modern consciousness" (Scollon and Scollon 1981; see Berger *et al.* 1973, as well). Modern consciousness is a viewpoint that holds (consciously or unconsciously) that "higher intelligence" is epitomized by explicitness (i.e. low reliance on context), analytic skills, logical (deductive) thought, abstract definitions and generalizations, and sustained attention to or communication on a single topic (see also Goody 1977; Goody and Watt 1963; Olson 1977; Ong 1982).

It is sometimes said, by people influenced by the Russian scholar Bakhtin (1981, 1986), that academic language, and its attendant form of consciousness, is

91

"monologic" and not dialogic. This is not quite right. All language is dialogic in the sense that it is designed to communicate with an "assumed other." Thus a person writing on a fan fiction site is assuming a particular type of reader – a fellow fan.

The "assumed other" for academic language, however, is a person who backgrounds his or her distinctive individual, social, ethnic, economic, and cultural properties, and in that sense fictionalizes him or herself (Scollon and Scollon 1981). This backgrounding is done in order that the person can take on the persona of a rational, generalizing, deductive, "generic," "disinterested," asocial and acultural pursuer of fact and truth. This is to say, such a person seeks to take on the very persona that is also the "voice" or "author" of academic language (by "voice" or "author" here I mean the "presumed author": that is, the persona one must adopt when speaking or writing academic language). In this sense, academic language both creates an "other" and then insists that the "other" be pretty much like the "author."

It is important for anyone interested in education to see that when it comes to the acquisition of any variety of academic language, there are both significant *losses* and *gains* (Halliday and Martin 1993). To see this, consider the two sentences below, which we also discussed in Chapter 2. The first (1) is in a vernacular variety of language and the second (2) is in an academic variety of language:

1   Hornworms sure vary a lot in how well they grow.
2   Hornworm growth exhibits a significant amount of variation.

Subjects of sentences name what a sentence is about (its "topic") and (when they are initial in the sentence) the perspective from which we are viewing the claims we want to make (the sentence's "theme"). The vernacular sentence above (1) is about hornworms (cute little green worms) and launches off from the perspective of the hornworm. The presence of "sure" helps to cause the subject here ("hornworms") also to be taken as naming a thing with which we are empathizing. The specialist sentence (2) is not about hornworms, but about a trait or feature of hornworms (in particular one that can be quantified) and launches off from this perspective. The cute little hornworm and our empathy for it disappears.

The vernacular sentence involves dynamic processes (changes) named by verbs ("vary," "grow"). People tend to care a good deal about changes and transformations, especially in things with which they emphasize. The specialist sentence turns these dynamic processes into abstract things ("variation," "growth") through a linguistic device known as "nominalization" (Halliday and Martin 1993). The dynamic changes disappear. We can also mention that the vernacular sentence has a contentful verb ("vary"), while the specialist one has a verb of appearance ("exhibit"), a class of verbs that is similar to copulas (i.e. verbs like "be") and are not as deeply or richly contentful as verbs like "vary." Such copulative verbs are basically just ways to relate things to each other (in this case abstract things, to boot).

The vernacular sentence has a quantity term ("how well") that is not just about amount or degree, but is also "telically evaluative," if I may be allowed to coin a term ("telos" means the ideal end-point or goal towards which something is striving). "How well" is both about a quantity and evaluates this amount in terms of an end-point or "telos" germane to hornworms: that is, in terms of a point of good or proper or full growth towards which hornworms are "meant" to move. Some hornworms reach the telos (end-point or goal) and others fall short. Humans, it turns out, care a lot about the end-points or goals of things. The specialist sentence replaces this "telically evaluative" term with a more precise measurement term that is "discipline evaluative" ("significant amount"). "Significant amount" is about an amount that is evaluated in terms of the goals and procedures of an academic discipline (here a type of biology), not a hornworm. It is a particular area of biology that determines what amounts to significant variation and what does not. All our hornworms could be stunted or atypical of well-grown hornworms ("well-grown" from a non-specialist everyday perspective) and still display a significant amount of variation in their sizes.

This last difference is related to another one: the vernacular sentence contains an appreciative marker ("sure"), while the specialist sentence leaves out such markers. The appreciative marker communicates the attitude, interest, and even values of the speaker/writer. Attitude, interest, and values, in this sense, are left out of the specialist sentence. One would not normally say or write "Hornworm growth sure exhibits a significant amount of variation" (if you don't know this, then you aren't at home with this sort of academic language).

So when one has to leave "everyday" (non-specialist) life to acquire and then use the specialist language above, these are some of the things that are lost: concrete things like hornworms and empathy for them; changes and transformations as dynamic ongoing processes; telos and appreciation. What is gained are: abstract things and relations among them; traits and quantification and categorization of traits; evaluation from within a specialized discipline. The crucial question then is this: *"Why would anyone – most especially a child in school – accept this loss?"*

My view is that people will accept this loss only if they see the gain *as a gain*. So a crucial question in science education, for example, ought to be: *"What would make someone see acquiring a scientific variety of language as a gain?"* Specialist languages are tied to socially situated identities and activities (i.e. people use them to do things while acting as certain kinds of people with characteristic viewpoints, values, and ways of acting, talking, and believing). People can only see a new specialist language as a gain if: (a) they recognize and understand the sorts of socially situated identities and activities that recruit the specialist language; (b) they value these identities and activities, or at least understand why they are valued; and (c) they believe they (will) have real access to these identities and activities, or at least (will) have access to meaningful (perhaps simulated) versions of them. Thus science in school is learned best and most deeply when it is, for the learner, about "being a scientist" (of some sort) "doing science" (of some sort). This is why video games are so good at getting learning done (Gee 2003). They allow people to be and do new things in new worlds, sometimes far beyond what they could be or do in the "real" world.

Thus acquisition is heavily tied at the outset to identity issues. It is tied to the learner's willingness and trust to leave (for a time and place) the "everyday" world and participate in another identity – one that for everyone represents a certain loss. For some people it represents a more significant loss in terms of a disassociation from, and even opposition to, their home- and community-based cultures. These cultures are not rooted in the sort of middle-class home-based cultures that have historically built up some sense of shared interests and values with some academic specialist domains (Finn 1999; Gee 1996 – see Chapter 3 above as well). For such people the issue is not just a lack of familiarity with the new identity (which is initially an issue for all learners). The issue is, as well, a feeling of opposition or hostility between the new identity they are being asked to assume and other identities they are already comfortable with. And of course in some cases this sense of hostility is historically accurate, since some academic domains (e.g. psychology) have historically denigrated certain sorts of people (e.g. people of color, women, and poor people; see Fausto-Sterling 1985; Gould 1981).

Academic language, aligned with "modern consciousness," today represents a family of "old literacies" (the various school-based and disciplinary-based practices that recruit some variety of oral and written academic language – and it's fair to use the term "literacy" here, since oral forms of academic language are different from, but related to, their written forms). They have been around now for some time. We have, for some time now, used them as our litmus test of school success and intelligence. Such literacies have by no means disappeared, nor will they. However, I would argue that academic language, and its attendant modern consciousness, once thought to be central to what counted as a "schooled" and "intelligent" person, is now at best a *necessary, but not sufficient* condition for success in society.

My argument here is not that acquiring facility with academic language ever guaranteed success in society, or necessarily mitigated the effects of racism, for example, but only that people often equated facility with academic language with "intelligence," modernity, and "being educated" (Goody and Watt 1963; Ong 1977; Olson 1977, 1994). Failing to acquire academic language may still bar poor and minority children from power in society, but acquiring academic language (and showing affiliation with school and school-based practices and values) is now at least joined by other important centers of action.

To get at where some of these other centers of action are, we will need to turn to "new literacies." Just as we educators are beginning to get a handle on the issues connected to poor and minority children acquiring the languages and identities connected to schooling, our new capitalist, high-tech, global world is changing the nature of identities at play in the world and their connections to literacies and knowledge.

The old and the new capitalism

The sort of capitalism we associate with the great economic success of the United States after World War II we can call the "old capitalism." It is the capitalism of large industries and assembly lines. The old capitalism (Drucker 1999; Kanigel 1997) is a social formation that has been transformed by our current high-tech, global world (see Castells 1996; Gee *et al.* 1996; Greider 1997; H. Smith 1995; Reich 1992). The old capitalism did not disappear; it still exists as a foregrounded formation in the "developing world" (where many of the developed worlds industrial jobs have "disappeared" to) and as a backgrounded formation in the "developed world" (Drucker 1999; Greider 1997).

Thanks to people like Fredrick Winslow Taylor (Kanigel 1997), work in the old capitalism came to be carried out at a pace and in terms of procedures determined by a "science" of efficiency, not by workers themselves. The craft knowledge of the workers (who had, before the Industrial Revolution, often worked at their own pace as craftspeople in their own shops and homes) was removed from the workers' heads and bodies and placed into the science of work, the rules of the workplace, and the knowledge of managers and bosses. A top-down system was created in terms of which knowledge and control existed at the top (the bosses) and not at the bottom (the workers). Middle managers conveyed and mediated knowledge, information, and control between the top and the bottom. This became, too, pretty much how knowledge was viewed in schools: knowledge was a system of expertise, owned by specialists, and imposed top-down on students.

"Taylorism" was actually an improvement. Capitalism prior to the twentieth century was often based on bosses enforcing their will on workers by intimidation backed up by laws that supported those bosses and not the workers. Taylor replaced the rule of force by "scientific" principles of efficiency that determined how work could be done most efficiently and effectively. Such principles would replace both the thuggery of the bosses and the craft knowledge of workers. Henry Ford's assembly line became the epitome of this process. Workers didn't think; they simply carried out pieces of a job – the whole of which they didn't understand – in the most routine and efficient way possible.

In a sense Taylorism "worked." It eventually made workers "middle class" as it spread the gains of productivity to much of society. What allowed a relatively peaceful "stand off" between workers and managers in the old capitalism was its great success in producing commodities (Rifkin 2000; Thurow 1999). Commodities are standardized products that become inexpensive enough to be widely available. Eventually even workers possessed many of the commodities – cars, televisions, refrigerators – that characterized a middle-class lifestyle at the economic level.

However, by the 1970s advances in science and technology allowed modern conditions of work and the mass production of commodities to be carried out successfully in a great variety of countries, even in some so-called "developing countries." The result was (and is) a global overproduction of commodities and hyper-competition for consumers and markets across the globe (Greider 1997; Thurow 1999). The production of commodities (which, of course, continues and will continue across the world) becomes a backgrounded part of the new economy: one that, in general, cannot reap great profits (unless one is first into a market with a new commodity).

In many cases jobs manufacturing commodities have moved to "developing" countries, where wages and constraints on things like pollution are low. In turn, developed countries have grown massive numbers of jobs requiring technical knowledge (so-called "knowledge work") and service jobs. Such jobs support the more profitable endeavors in the new capitalism, namely the creation of technical knowledge and the provision of personal services to well-off people.

In the new capitalism the biggest profits come not from commodities (which are cheap and can be produced anywhere – so there's lots of competition), but from designing new services, new products, and new knowledge for different niches, markets, and lifestyles. Often people buy such services, knowledge, or products not based on price, but on the status they are associated with. Think of the upper-middle-class parents driving down the road in their tank-like Hummer taking their middle-school child to his or her once-weekly meeting with a counselor who helps prepare the child to get into an elite private college. The family is not cost-conscious about the Hummer, the counselor, or the college. Furthermore, while low-priced cars are still a commodity (one produced throughout the world now), Hummers and other niche vehicles are not (they are well out of the reach of most people).

There is another result as well: many workers cease to be "middle class" (Beck 2000). The new industrial worker, and the many other sorts of non-middle-class workers to which the new capitalism gives rise, especially temporary and service workers, can no longer afford to live in the sorts of communities, or to live with the degree of stability and security, that made workers in the old capitalism feel securely middle class (Rifkin 1995). This is despite the fact that, in the new capitalism, workers are often asked to think and act more proactively in the business's interest: there is a movement to place the sorts of knowledge and control normally reserved for middle managers back into worker's heads and bodies (whence Taylor had taken them) (Drucker 1999). In turn this has imperiled many middle managers, whose knowledge and supervisory tasks can readily be taken over by front-line workers.

Putting knowledge back into the workers' heads allows the worker to do what the old worker and the middle manager used to do, thereby making the workforce "lean and mean" in a highly competitive age. In modern auto assembly plants the workers work in teams that carry out a whole process, rather than (as in the old capitalism) each individual doing a meaningless piece of the process, disconnected from each other. Workers meet in "quality circles" to discuss how to transform their work to make it better. The worker can stop the assembly line; there is no need to wait for a boss to make the decision. On the other hand, many auto workers are out of work, their jobs replaced by robots.

Much work in the new capitalism involves teams and collaboration, based on the idea that in a fast-changing environment, where knowledge goes out of date rapidly and technological innovation is common, a team can behave more smartly than any individual in it by pooling and distributing knowledge. Furthermore, in the new capitalism work is more and more *project-based* (Gee *et al.* 1996; H. Smith 1995). A team comes together to carry out a project, and when the project changes or is over the team reassembles and many of its members move on to other projects in the same business or other ones. Security in the new capitalism, such as it is, is rooted not in jobs and wages, but in what I will call one's "portfolio." By one's portfolio I mean the skills, achievements, and previous experiences that a person owns and that he or she can arrange and rearrange to sell him or herself for new opportunities in changed times.

Identities

So if commodities are not central to the new capitalism, what is? The answer, I believe, is *design* (Kress *et al.* 2001; Kress and Van Leeuwen 2001; New London Group 1996). There are three types of design that reap large rewards in the new capitalism: the ability to design new *identities*, *affinity spaces*, and *networks*. These three types are all deeply interrelated (Gee 2000–1). In turn, people who are adept at taking on new identities, adept at using and interacting within affinity spaces, and are well connected in networks will flourish.

Let's start with designed *identities*. One type of design typical in the new capitalism (Rifkin 2000) is the ability to design products, services, or experiences so that they create or take advantage of a specific identity connected to specific sorts of consumers (and one and the same individual might constitute several different types of consumer). In turn, businesses seek through the design of such identities to contract an ongoing *relationship* with the consumer in terms of which he or she can be sold ever newer variations on products and services or from which information can be leveraged for sale to other businesses. The product or service itself is not the important element here. After all, many products (as commodities) are getting cheaper and cheaper to make (as the cost of materials – and especially computer chips – gets lower and lower) and many services don't involve any material things at all (Thurow 1999). What is important is the identity and relationship that are associated with the product or service.

Let me give just one example, typical of a myriad of others. Consider the website palm.com, the site of the Palm™ company, which sells handheld computer organizers. A series of rotating pictures at the top of the site clearly signals the sort of identity the company wants the consumer to assume (e.g. "Find yourself on the road to independence," associated with a picture of the open road, or "Find yourself on the road to freedom," associated with a picture of downhill skiing, or

"Follow Wall Street from your street," associated with a picture of the Wall Street sign). Furthermore, the site contains a link to the "The Palm Community," where consumers can swap stories, chat with other Palm users, contribute to a discussion board, give advice to other users, get information on related products and links, download free software, and sign up for a free email newsletter. The Palm™ company is contracting an ongoing relationship with their consumers, placing them in relationship to (networking them with) each other, and creating an affinity group (see next section).

Affinity spaces

Let me now turn to designing *affinity spaces*. As I argued in Chapter 6, affinity spaces are increasingly important today, both in business and politics (Beck 1999; Beck *et al.* 1994; Rifkin 2000). Greens, Saturn owners, members of an elite guarded-gate community, users of Amazon.com, skate boarders, poetry rave fans, or Pokémon fanatics all have affinity spaces within which they share practices, patterns of consumption, and ongoing relationships to specific businesses and organizations. An affinity space is a place (physical, virtual, or a mixture of the two) wherein people interact with each other, often at a distance (that is, not necessarily face-to-face, though face to face interactions can also be involved), primarily through shared practices or a common endeavor (which entails shared practices), and only secondarily through shared culture, gender, ethnicity, or face-to-face relationships (see Rose 1997 for an important discussion of the relationships between affinity spaces as a contemporary form of organization and activism and social class). People are brought together through a shared affinity for a common goal, endeavor, or interest, not first and foremost because they are "bonded" to each other personally (which is why we wanted, in Chapter 6, to replace the term "community").

In an affinity space knowledge is often both *intensive* (each person entering the space brings some special knowledge) and *extensive* (each person entering the space shares some knowledge and functions with others). In an affinity space knowledge is also often *distributed* across people, tools, and technologies, not held in any one person or thing, and *dispersed*: that is people in the space, using modern information and communication technologies, can draw on knowledge in sites outside the space itself. (Though, thanks to modern technology, in a sense nothing is really outside the space. It's all a matter of links in a network.)

Finally, in an affinity space much knowledge is often *tacit*: that is, built up by daily practice and stored in the routines and procedures of the people who use the space. Such knowledge is not easily verbally explicated. New members acquire such tacit knowledge by guided participation in the practices of the space, not primarily through direct instruction outside the practice. The guidance they receive comes not only from more advanced users of the space, but also from various objects, tools, and technologies found in the space, many of which are designed to facilitate and supplement users' knowledge and skills.

Networks

Finally, let me turn to designing *networks*. Another crucial aspect of design in the new capitalism is *networking* people and organizations (Kelly 1998). Networking involves designing communicational links between people and organizations. It also crucially involves creating links between people and various sorts of tools and technologies. These tools and technologies not only help create the communicational links that constitute networks; they are themselves nodes in the network in which knowledge is stored and across which it is distributed (together with people's minds).

In fast-changing times and markets the more nodes to which one is connected the more information one receives and the faster one can adapt and change. Networks harness the power of *unfamiliarity*. If people or organizations are networked only with people or organizations like themselves, then everyone in the network pretty much knows what everyone else knows and there is nothing very new to be learned. In slow-changing times, this is fine – maybe even good – since a common core of knowledge can be ever refined. On the other hand, if people or organizations are networked with diverse others, then they are going to learn and keep learning new things – things not already in their own repertoire of knowledge and skills. In a fast-changing world, the power of network links to unfamiliar people and organizations is crucial.

Networks that leverage the power of unfamiliarity often have to be large and diffuse, and many of the links are relatively weak links, unlike the strong bonds that people tend to have with those with whom they are familiar and with whom they share a good deal. We come more and more to live in a world of many weak links, rather than a few strong ones. This is aided and abetted by the increased *mobility* of many people in the new capitalism: people who move, either physically or virtually, from place to place, creating multiple diffuse weak links to other people and organizations (Bauman 1998). In fact, in the new capitalist world, mobility is a form and source of power. The mobile classes often leave it to the locals (people who cannot get out or who have few links beyond their area) to clean up (or live with) the messes they have left behind.

Millennials

There is a generation of children today who have lived their entire lives in the new capitalism. These children are part of a new baby boom – a generation that has been called by many names: e.g. Generation Y, Generation XX, Echo Boom, Generation Next, the Bridger Generation, Generation 2K, Millennials, and so forth (Howe and Strauss 2000; O'Reilly 2000). At the earliest, these children were born in 1982 (and this only for the United States, where the trends that gave rise to Millennials happened earlier than elsewhere – in other places in the world they are not yet in their teens; see Howe and Strauss 2000: ch. 13).

One interesting way to begin to get at the different sensibilities of many (though of course, not all) Millennials in comparison to Baby Boomers (people like myself who were initially socialized within the old capitalism and lived through the upheavals of the 1960s and the chaotic dawning of the new capitalism) is to look at the television programs that are helping to socialize the Millennials. Many Baby Boomers can't stand shows like *Barney & Friends* and *Blue's Clues*, but they rather like *Sesame Street*. Young Millennials like *Sesame Street*, especially the Muppets, but they also like *Barney* and *Blue's Clues*, often more than *Sesame Street*.

Let me take a moment to contrast *Sesame Street* (first aired in 1969) with *Barney & Friends* (first aired in 1991) and *Blue's Clues* (which within months of its first airing in 1996 was trouncing *Sesame Street* in the ratings, see Gladwell 2000: ch. 3). The themes that emerge from this analysis, by and large, replicate themes that emerge from a contrast between the Baby Boomer generation and the Millennial generation, a topic to which I will turn briefly in a moment. Below, I reprint material from the shows' websites about their respective philosophies. I have italicized words that I believe are particularly important for the following discussion:

Sesame Street

http://www.sesameworkshop.org/faq/answers/0,6113,0,00.html
designed to use the medium of television to reach and teach pre-schoolers, and give them *skills* that would provide a *successful transition from home to school*. The show gave children *a head start* and provided them with enough *confidence* to begin learning the *alphabet, numbers, and pro-social skills* ... Everything about the series was a departure from previous children's television programming – from its format to its *focus on disadvantaged inner city children*, to the way it *combined education and entertainment*.

Barney & Friends

http://www.pbs.org/barney/html/Philosophy.html
The programs are designed to *enhance the development of the whole child* – the cognitive, social, emotional, and physical domains ... A strong emphasis is put on *prosocial skills* such as making friends, sharing, cooperating, and using good manners.

Blue's Clues

http://www.nickjr.com/grownups/home/shows/blue/blues_play_to_learn.jhtml
Play-to-learn is the essence of *Blue's Clues*. *Blue's Clues* was created to *celebrate the life of a preschooler* – who they are, what they know, and how they experience and learn from everything that they do ... Every episode is developed to fulfill the mission of the show: to *empower*, *challenge*, and *build the self-esteem* of preschoolers all the while making them laugh.

Sesame Street is devoted to the transition from home to school, especially in respect to "disadvantaged inner city children." Note that "pro-social skills" for *Sesame Street* are part of a list of school-based things like literacy (the alphabet) and numeracy (numbers). "Pro-social" here appears to mean "knowing how to behave in school." *Sesame Street* is, in many respects, a quite overt form of early schooling, a kind of Head Start program all of its own.

Sesame Street combines real people and Muppets in an urban-looking three-dimensional space. It is replete with an often wryly humorous subtext directed at adults (e.g. Monsterpiece Theater) and uses a good deal of metaphorical language and language play that only adults can understand. *Sesame Street* displays, foregrounds, and celebrates social and cultural differences. In fact, the celebration of difference is one of its major themes.

Barney & Friends is not primarily about making the transition from home to school, though it embeds in its shows things like counting or learning shapes. It is primarily about the "whole child" and "prosocial skills" in the sense of cooperation and community, not in the sense of knowing how to behave in school per se. It contains a good deal of play, song, dance, and other sorts of movement of the body, and less school-type language than *Sesame Street*. Like *Sesame Street* it combines real people and fantasy figures, but in a suburban, or even rural, context, not an urban one.

Barney & Friends has little or no subtext directed at adults and engages in little or no metaphorical language of the sort only an adult could understand. While *Barney & Friends* displays children of different ethnic groups, it does not foreground social or cultural differences. Rather, one of its major themes is commonality and what makes children the same.

Blue's Clues (in which children solve a puzzle using three clues in each episode) takes *Barney & Friends* one step further. It is overtly about "playing to learn," much like *Barney*, which often seems to be about "singing and dancing around to learn," and thus in a sense overtly juxtaposes itself over against or contrasts itself with school (which is not to say it is anti-school). It celebrates the life of a preschooler and what preschoolers are and know as they are now, not as they will become in the future. It is about "empowerment," where "empowerment" means feeling smart and being willing to take on intellectual challenges.

Blue's Clues combines one real person (originally "Steve," now gone from the show) with fantasy. Like *Barney*, it is filmed in a setting that looks suburban or even rural, but the setting is two-dimensional. It looks like a child's magazine or book in bright primary colors, not like the real world (e.g. the dog "Blue" looks like a cut-out of a child's drawing of a blue dog).

Blue's Clues entirely eschews adult-directed subtext and metaphorical language. Characters are named quite literally (e.g. "Blue," a dog that is blue; "Shovel," a shovel; "Pail," a pail). The host often directly faces the camera and interacts with the show's child viewers, giving them ample time to answer his queries and comments. While *Blue's Clues* very occasionally shows culturally diverse children (it rarely shows any humans besides the host), it has next to nothing to do with difference, diversity, or commonality. It is primarily focused on the socially situated cognitive growth of children in interaction with an adult and his cognitive "mediating devices" – characters like Blue, Shovel, Pail, and Soap, as well as tools like a notebook in which to keep a record of the clues, all of which help the child solve the problems (see the interview with Alice Wilder, director of research for *Blue's Clues*, who makes it clear that the show has been influenced by recent theories of situated cognition, at http://www.nickjr.com/grownups/home/shows/blue/inside/alice_wilder_interview.jhtml).

Sesame Street is designed to entice the parent to watch with the child, assuming the parent (perhaps a poor disadvantaged urban mother) might not. *Sesame Street* assumes (certain) kids need a head start for school – a head start they may not get in their homes (perhaps poor disadvantaged urban homes). *Barney* and *Blue's Clues* do nothing to entice the parent to watch, but their websites make it clear that they absolutely assume a parent is watching with the child, and in an interactive way. Unlike *Sesame Street*, *Barney* and *Blue's Clues* assume parents are so devoted to their children's interests and development (in the case of *Blue's Clues* especially their intellectual development) that they do not need a subtext to keep them attending with their child. *Barney* and *Blue's Clues* do not assume that children need a head start for school. Rather they assume children will develop through play and that they have homes that will enhance their smartness and add value to their play.

Sesame Street assumes that what children really need they will or ought to get in school or through schooling. It does not compete with school; rather it prepares children for school. *Barney & Friends* takes place alongside school and is a space that enhances school and schooling. When *Barney* shows a classroom, it always seems so inert; the displays and activities left over from the school day only really come alive when Barney and the children enact them into communal song and dance after school. *Blue's Clues* is in a space (Steve's two-dimensional home) completely away from school and, in a sense, it is in competition with school. In many respects, it is better than school. Steve's home, like many of the homes of the children watching *Blue's Clues*, seems to assume that it has a truer sense of who children are and what they know and need than does school.

Sesame Street, on the one hand, and *Barney & Friends* and *Blue's Clues* on the other, orient quite differently towards literacy. *Sesame Street* overtly stresses and show-cases language, literacy, and school skills. *Barney & Friends* does not stress these things, but rather stresses the body, play, the whole child, sharing, and commonality. *Blue's Clues* also does not stress language, literacy, or schooling, but rather stresses thinking, problem-solving, and empowerment. In *Barney & Friends* and *Blue's Clues* children become literate and smart by being and celebrating themselves. In *Sesame Street* they become literate and smart by learning school-based skills.

Blue's Clues is, in my view, the ultimate Millennial show for small children. Its practices and values are fully aligned with rhetoric about new capitalist work-places (Drucker 1999; Gee *et al.* 1996). New capitalist workplaces (according to this rhetoric) require empowered employees who can think for themselves and who think of themselves as smart and creative people. They require employees who are good at problem-solving and who can use various tools and technologies to solve problems. In turn, *Barney & Friends* celebrates things like working together (think of work teams and quality circles) and commonality and community (think of corporate cultures and communities of practice) so commonly stressed in the literature on new capitalist workplaces.

Barney & Friends and *Blue's Clues* are also well aligned with the current practices and views of homes attuned to the new capitalism. Such homes see school as only one site – and perhaps not the most important one – for enriching and accelerating their children (Gee and Crawford 1998; Gee 2000; Gee *et al.* 2001). Such homes offer their children a plethora of out-of-school tools, technologies, experiences, activities, and sites for the formation of intellectual and social skills that will equip them for elite higher education and success in the new capitalist world. In line with current neoliberal philosophy, homes that cannot leverage such advantages for their children in the free marketplace are entitled only to the basic skills that "accountable" public schools have to offer "off market" (this argument is made overtly in D'Souza 2001).

Boomers vs. Millennials

Having talked about some of the shows shaping Millennial children, let me now turn to what popular sources have had to say about the contrasts between Baby Boomers (when they were younger) and Millennials (18 at the oldest, but with the heart of their generation younger). I cannot go into details here, but suffice it to say that the "big picture" is something like what I sketch below (Howe and Strauss 2000; O'Reilly 2000; http://millennialsrising.com/survey.shtml). Keep in mind that I am telling here a story that applies to well-off children better than to others, though it does apply to many others as well, thanks in part to the way the Internet and modern media allow trends to spread (and standardize) quickly across diverse groups. In fact the children who express the Millennial trends I discuss below serve as something of an "attractor" for others in their generation (which does not mean that one effect of this is not resistance).

So here's the story: many Millennials regret the societal fragmentation and extreme individualism to which the Boomers' earlier assault (in the 1960s and 1970s) on social and governmental institutions gave rise. However, Millennials live in a new capitalist world in which the gap between the poor and the rich has increased. This growing gap has been caused by the very logic of the new capitalism – a logic of increasing returns or a "winner take all" system (Frank and Cook 1995). By and large, many Millennials appear to find this logic acceptable, natural, and inevitable (Gee 2000; Gee *et al.* 2001; Rifkin 2000).

In the new capitalism, the increase of technological and scientific innovations, the rise of immigration, increases in global trade, and the ability of businesses to get workers at the lowest price across the globe have widened the market-determined difference between high and low wages (Greider 1997; Thurow 1999). Over the Millennial childhood, Millennials have seen workers with high educational credentials gain more and more income, while they have seen poor people and immigrants fill unskilled labor positions and the massive supply of service jobs.

All this has created something of a paradox for the Millennials. They want to stress commonality, community, conformity, responsibility, and civic duties, while they also want to accept as natural large disparities between the rich and the poor, even to the point of accepting as natural the existence, power, and status of an overclass. Of course this paradox exists in large part because Millennials have seen Baby Boomers in their Yuppie guise (attained when many of them gave up their 1960s rebellion for success in the Reagan neoliberal frontier) come to accept and even celebrate this overclass themselves (Howe and Strauss 2000: p. 109).

The acceptance and importance of this overclass is, perhaps, one reason many parents today seek to control their children's time and attention so tightly (Millennials show a significant decline in the amount of time they spend in unstructured activity compared to Gen-Xers as children; see Howe and Strauss 2000: pp. 134, 170–2). Such parents feel they must heavily invest in and control their children if they are to end up successful in the hour-glass social structure that constitutes the new capitalism (lots of rich and poor at the top and bottom, and fewer and more vulnerable people in the middle).

It is interesting that polls show that even well-off Millennials like school less with each passing year, but accept it as necessary for their future (Public Agenda 1997; Howe and Strauss 2000: pp. 162, 166, 182). Many Millennials see success in school as necessary for the future precisely because they (and their parents) are aware of the role that educational credentials, especially from elite institutions, play in the new capitalist world. At the same time they are well aware that many of the core credentials, skills, experiences, and identities necessary for success in that world are not gained in school, but rather outside school at home, in activities, camps, travel, and on the Net.

In terms of how Millennials answer surveys, diversity appears to function quite differently for them than it did for the Baby Boomers (Howe and Strauss 2000: ch. 10). The Baby Boomers lived in a world in which the great divide was between black and white and race was the key social issue. In the world in which Millennials live diversity doesn't mean black or white; it means a great many shades of white, brown, and black: Chinese, Vietnamese, Koreans, Japanese, Malaysians, Asian-Americans, Mexicans, Mexican-Americans, Indians, Guatemalans, El Salvadorians, Colombians, Peruvians, etc. and etc. through a very long list indeed (and each of these groups comes in many types, income levels, and colors). This is not to claim that race is not objectively crucial in the world still, only that, at least according to surveys, Millennials answer in ways that seem to show that they pay less attention to race (in terms of black and white) than do (or did) Baby Boomers, and more attention to a wider array of types of diversity.

In the Millennials' world, segregation is increasing, both in communities and schools (and on television, where blacks and whites now watch quite different shows). But for the Millennials segregation is defined more by income than race

(Howe and Strauss 2000: p. 220). Boomer and Gen-X parents appear to have less and less interest in raising their children in multicultural settings, in part because, while they tend to accept cultural diversity as a value and still care about civil rights, they do not want their children mixing with poor children of any sort.

Gender works differently for Millennials as well (Howe and Strauss 2000: Ch. 10; Gilbert and Gilbert 1998). In schools girls, in nearly every area, are showing more progress than boys. In fact some colleges are beginning to see fewer and less good applications from boys, and more boys dropping out. Even in areas like math and science where boys are still ahead of girls, the girls are fast catching up. Girls appear to be the cultural leading edge of the Millennials, with many Millennial boys caught between following the lead of the girls or retaining the behaviors of Gen-Xers.

Shape-shifting portfolio people

The new capitalist literature calls for what I have elsewhere referred to as "shape-shifting portfolio people" (Gee 1999b, 2000). Shape-shifting portfolio people are people who see themselves in entrepreneurial terms. That is, they see themselves as free agents in charge of their own selves as if those selves were projects or businesses. They believe they must manage their own risky trajectories through building up a variety of skills, experiences, and achievements in terms of which they can define themselves as successful now and worthy of more success later. Their set of skills, experiences, and achievements, at any one time, constitutes their portfolio. However, they must also stand ready and able to rearrange these skills, experiences, and achievements creatively (that is, to shape-shift into different identities) in order to define themselves anew (as competent and worthy) for changed circumstances. If I am now an "X," and the economy no longer needs "X"s, or "X"s are no longer the right thing to be in society, but now "Y"s are called for, then I have to be able to shape-shift quickly into a "Y."

In earlier work I have argued that well-off teens today see home, community, school, and society in just such terms (Gee 1999b, 2000; Gee *et al.* 2001). They seek to pick up a variety of experiences (e.g. the "right" sort of summer camps, travel, and special activities), skills (not just school-based skills, but a wide variety of interactional, aesthetic, and technological skills), and achievements (honors, awards, projects) in terms of which they can define themselves as worthy of admission to elite educational institutions and worthy of professional success later in life. They think and act, from quite early in life, in terms of their "résumé." Note that school (or at least the classroom at school) is not the only, perhaps not even the central, site for filling up one's résumé.

Shape-shifting did not start with the Millennials. In fact, as the old capitalism gradually turned into the new, and neoliberalism became hegemonic in much of the Western world, there were calls for such people (e.g. Boyett and Conn 1992; Drucker 1989; Handy 1989; Peters 1987), many of them caused by the success of Japan in the 1980s. Of course at the time this often meant adults were being asked to think of themselves in new ways. On the other hand, the Millennials are a generation in which there are wide-scale expectations, at least among many middle- and upper-middle-class families, that children will think of themselves and build themselves in this way from the earliest ages. The old capitalism left a good deal of space for someone to enter the middle class without being a shape-shifting portfolio person (think of all the secure union jobs that paid middle-class wages). The new capitalism leaves much less space in this regard.

Class means something different in the new capitalism than it did in the old. In the old capitalism there was a broad and massive "middle class" defined by one's ability to consume standardized commodities. In the new capitalism class is defined by the nature of one's portfolio, the sorts of experiences, skills, and achievements one has accrued (which one shares, by and large, with the "right" sort of people) and one's ability to manage these in a shape-shifting way. One's portfolio surely correlates with one's parents' income (though by no means perfectly), but what matters is the portfolio and the way in which it is viewed and managed. If you have no portfolio or don't view yourself in portfolio terms, then you are at risk in the new capitalism.

Diverse Millennials

To many it may seem as if my talk of Millennials only applies to well-off young people, perhaps even only well-off white young people. However, lots of young people today who are not well-off or white display Millennial viewpoints and aspirations. Let me briefly discuss but one example. Wan Shun Eva Lam in her excellent article "L2 literacy and the design of the self" (2000: all page numbers following are to this article) discusses a case that is not at all untypical in a Millennial generation, 35 percent of whom are non-white or Latino (Howe and Strauss 2000: p. 83).

Lam's focal student, whom she calls "Almon," emigrated at the age of 12 from Hong Kong to the United States. After five years in the USA, Almon was frustrated by his skills in English. School only offered him ESL (English as a second language), bilingual, or remedial courses, which stigmatized him as a "low-achieving student" (p. 466). Almon felt that it was going to be hard for him to develop his "career" (his word, p. 467) in the United States because of his English skills. However, eventually Almon got involved with the Internet, created his own personal home page on a Japanese pop singer, "compiled a long list of names of on-line chat mates in several countries around the world, and was starting to write regularly to a few e-mail 'pen pals'" (p. 467). Almon's Internet writing eventually improved his writing in school significantly.

After his experiences with and on the Net, here is how Almon talked about himself and his future:

> I'm not as fearful, or afraid of the future, that I won't have a future . . .
> [my ellipsis, JPG] I didn't feel I belonged to this world . . . But now I feel

106

there's nothing to be afraid of. It really depends on how you go about it. It's not like the world always has power over you. It was [names of a few chat mates and email pen pals] who helped me to change and encouraged me. If I hadn't known them, perhaps I wouldn't have changed so much . . . Yeah, maybe the *Internet* has changed me.

(p. 468)

Almon had chosen to settle his home page in the "Tokyo" section of *GeoCities* (an international server) where a global group of Asians (of all different sorts) gathers around Japanese pop culture. Almon's online chat mates were located in a wide variety of places, such as Canada, Hong Kong, Japan, Malaysia, and the United States.

Almon's story is one variety of a typical Millennial story. He thinks in terms of his career and future and evaluates his current skills and experiences in that light. He gains his most important skills, experiences, and identities, including even school-based skills, outside of school (indeed school stigmatizes and deskills him). Though I have not discussed the matter above, Lam makes it clear that Almon's pen pal relationships are mainly with girls and that his remarks take on some of the values and perspectives that these girls enact on the Net (see pp. 473–4). Finally, he forms his new identities as part and parcel of an affinity group.

Lam argues that the genre of electronic dialogue, as a form of communication that relies heavily on writing, "constitutes a highly visible medium for the scripting of social roles" (p. 474). She points out that many of Almon's postings to his female interlocutors "sound both very personal and very much like role play". Almon not only gains new skills and develops new identities on the Net, he also learns to shape-shift: to enact different social roles by designing representations of meaning and self through language and other symbol systems, e.g. music, graphics, emoticons (New London Group 1996).

There is no doubt that Almon, regardless of his economically based social class, is building a portfolio and learning to think of himself in entrepreneurial terms (in the creation of his own website and in his sense of free agency and control over his own destiny) and in shape-shifting terms. Connected in an affinity-space way as he is to a young Asian diaspora, many of whom are, rich or poor, core Millennials, Almon is not at the margins (except in the eyes of the school), but at the center of the new capitalist world.

A note on learning in the new capitalist world

One important theme in the world in which Millennials are growing up is, I believe, this: thanks to modern technology, young people today are often exposed outside of school to processes of learning that are deeper and richer than the forms of learning to which they are exposed in schools. I do not have space here to develop this theme very fully. Let me give but one example of what I mean.

In recent work (Gee 2003), I have been investigating the principles of learning that are built into video and computer games. Video and computer games are today a major cultural practice of young people – the video and computer games industry now outsells the movie industry (Poole 2000). Video and computer games are prototypical high-tech products of the new capitalism, and the businesses that make them, in a highly competitive market, cannot have lots of people fail when they try to learn to play them (just as the makers of *Blue's Clues* have to get their research about what children want and can do right or go out of business).

Taking modern first- and third-person shooter games as an example (e.g. *Half-Life, Metal Gear Solid, Deus Ex, System Shock 2*), here are just a few (there are many more) of the learning principles that the player is (however tacitly) exposed to in learning to play these games. Learning is based on situated practice; there are lowered consequences for failure and taking risks (you've saved the game and can start over); learning is a form of extended engagement of self as an extension of an identity to which the player is committed; the learner can customize the game to suit his or her style of learning; the learning domain (e.g. a training module connected to the game) is a simplified subdomain of the real game; problems are ordered so that the first ones to be solved in the game lead to fruitful generalizations about how to solve more complex problems later; explicit information/ instruction is given "on demand" and "just in time" in the game world; learning is interactive (probing, assessing, and re-probing the world); there are multiple routes to solving a problem; there are intrinsic rewards (within the game) keyed to any player's level of expertise; the game operates at the outer edge of one's "regime of competence" (always doable with the resources you have at that point, never too easy); "basic skills" are not separated from higher-order skills – both are picked up bottom-up by playing the game or several different games of a given type or genre; the meaning of texts and symbols is situated in what one does, and is thus never purely verbal or textual; meaning/knowledge is built up through various modalities (images, texts, symbols, interactions, abstract design, sound, etc); meaning/knowledge is distributed between the player's mind, the objects and environments in the game world, and other players (who help); knowledge is dispersed as players go online to get help and discuss strategy; players use affinity spaces dedicated to a particular game or type of game for learning; the game constitutes a complex designed system and the player orients his or her learning to issues of design and the understanding of complex systems.

I could go on, but the point I hope is clear: imagine young people who have been immersed in this sort of learning coming to school to acquire academic language top-down in a setting remote from practice or affinity groups. Such young people experience much better viewpoints on learning in their "trivial" (from a Baby Boomer's perspective) cultural pursuits than they do in the schools Baby Boomers largely control. I should mention, too, that while school-based Baby Boomers give lip service to multicultural diversity and understanding, they rarely extend this understanding to the generational, peer-based, and popular cultures of the young people in school.

At the same time, it is clear that some of the learning principles I have just sketched are often integral to good science instruction (diSessa 2000), when such instruction seeks conceptual understanding and not just rote memory of facts. Such learning principles are also supported by a good deal of modern work in cognitive science concerned with how humans learn best (Kirshner and Whitson 1997). They are supported, as well, in much contemporary work on literacy learning that stresses critical and conceptual learning (Freedman *et al.* 1999; Rose 1999). On the other hand, they are just the sorts of principles that are driven out of schools by our current mania for testing and accountability.

Schools and schooling in the new capitalism

The notion of *experience* has become crucial in the new capitalist world. Shape-shifting portfolio people leverage distinctive experiences to form their portfolios and to underwrite their claims to distinction. New capitalist businesses often see themselves as primarily selling experiences (and relationships) customized to different consumer identities (Rifkin 2000). Current cognitive science of the sort based on situated cognition argues that people primarily reason, not by logical computations and on the basis of abstract generalizations, but by manipulating records of their actual experiences (Barsalou 1999a, b; Glenberg 1997; Gee 1992 – and remember, *Blue's Clues* is explicitly based on such work in cognitive science). You are what you have experienced, and in the new capitalist world distinctive experiences are for sale.

In general, outside of certain narrow spheres (e.g. science), the new capitalism has no great use for the persona of a rational, generalizing, deductive, "generic," "disinterested," asocial and acultural pursuer of fact and truth – the persona so central to the old capitalism and modern consciousness (Bauman 1992). Rather it values distinctive identities and skills rooted in distinctive and various (but often class-bound) experiences. At the same time, the new capitalism has no great use for – perhaps even a fear of – diversity centered in ethnic, cultural, and gender differences when these are not defined in terms of market niches. The diversity the new capitalism revels in is the sort of diversity defined by affinity spaces and networks centered in practices that markets create, transform, and sustain. And, in the new capitalism, these are affinity spaces and networks defined by socially and economically distinctive types of knowledge, information, skills, experiences, and lifestyles.

The great barrier today for many poor and minority children (those who come to school without the home-based head start for formal schooling that more affluent children often have), as I see it, is that mastery of academic language and affiliation with school-based values is necessary for success in the new capitalist world, but now this is only a small part of the whole picture. At the same time, the recent standards, testing, and accountability regime has committed schools to supplying all children, especially poor children, with no more (and no less) than "the basics." This of course fits perfectly with the neoliberal philosophy that underlies the new capitalism.

According to neoliberal philosophy, everything should be on a (free) market and people ought to get what (and only what) they can pay for (Hayek 1996; Sowell 1996; von Mises 1997). If, for humane reasons, there has to be, within a given area, something "off market" (i.e. free or subsidized), then it must be "basic," otherwise it will encourage people away from the market and disrupt it.

This of course allows children to begin to fill up their portfolios only if they can draw on family, community, or Internet resources, resources from various sorts of private sites and institutions, and school resources now often at the margins of the neoliberal central curriculum (in privileged public schools or private schools – private schools experienced a major increase in enrollment in the 1990s – and in special activities and programs at school). In turn, it leaves children without such resources to fill the huge number of service jobs created by the new capitalism and its distinctive workings of class defined in terms of the consumption of status and lifestyle. In the end, we get the Tale of Two Millennial Cities (Howe and Strauss 2000: p. 109) – a tale not of race, nor of class in traditional terms, but of "kinds of people" – those with and without portfolios, those with small and big portfolios, shape-shifters and non-shape-shifters.

It has not been my intention here to make recommendations for the future. Nonetheless, it seems to me that, for those who care about disadvantaged children, there are two possible courses of action (not necessarily mutually exclusive). One is to give up on public schools, accept their neoliberal function of delivering "the basics" accountably, and work to provide portfolio-forming activities and experiences, as well as political-critical capacities, for disadvantaged children outside of school and at school at the margins of the neoliberal curriculum. The other is to fight the neoliberal agenda and make schools sites for creativity, deep thinking, and the formation of whole people: sites in which all children can gain portfolios suitable for success, but success defined in multiple ways, and gain the ability to critique and transform social formations in the service of creating better worlds for all.

Bakhtinian thoughts

The Russian scholar Mikhail Bakhtin (1981, 1986) captures powerfully how spoken and written words always have two "sources." One source is the whole set of former utterances, texts, and institutions that have always already given those words meanings in culture and history. The other source is the individual person speaking or writing here and now, projecting onto the words his or her own "slant," and thereby adding to the cultural and historical possibilities of those words. And the same is true not just of words but of any other signs or symbols, whether they be images, artifacts, graphs, or what have you.

I have nothing novel to add to Bakhtin scholarship. But, nonetheless, I am inspired here by Bakhtin to meditate for just a moment on how one contemporary activity – namely video and computer games – might illuminate some of the ways in which the dynamic between these two sources of meaning works out, especially in our "new times." Video and computer games are now as influential in the popular culture of young people as are (or were) movies and books (Poole 2000). It is interesting to note that Bakhtin gained many of his insights about language at work in the world from a close study of narration and dialogue in novels. Perhaps we can gain some insights from video and computer games as well.

I will focus my discussion on a game named *Arcanum: Of Steamworks and Magick Obscura*. This is a game that takes place in a (virtual) world where once upon a time magic ("magick") ruled, but where technology has now arrived and magic and machines coexist in an uneasy balance. A variety of different groups – Humans, Elves, Gnomes, Dwarves, Orcs, and Ogres, as well as Half-Elves, Half-Orcs, and Half-Ogres (each of which have one Human parent) – cohabit this world, each orienting to the conflicts between magic and technology in different ways.

Before you start playing *Arcanum*, you must construct your character. Each group and gender has different natural characteristics. For example, each group and gender has its own unique degrees of strength, constitution, dexterity, beauty, intelligence, willpower, perception, and charisma (there are no real inequalities here, just differences – a character from any group you choose can fare well or poorly in the world of Arcanum). Each of these traits will affect how your character (i.e. you) carries out dialogue and action in the world of Arcanum and how other characters in the world respond.

When the game starts you also get five "points" that you can choose to distribute, in any way you wish, to your character, thereby changing his or her "natural" state (for example, a female Half-Elf has a natural strength of 7, but you could use one or more of your five points to make her stronger; the same goes for her other traits). As the game progresses and you gain more worldly experience through various actions in the game, you gain yet more points to distribute, thereby allowing your character to develop in certain ways and not others. These initial and subsequent points can be distributed to your character's primary traits such as strength and dexterity, but they can also be used to build up a wide variety of other skills, such as ability with a bow and arrow, skill in picking locks, or persuasive skills. They can be used to build up ability to cast a wide variety of magic spells or, instead, ability to build a wide variety of technological apparatus. You can choose to have a character primarily oriented to magic or technology or some mixture of the two. By the time you finish *Arcanum*, moving through many quests and interactions, your character is very different from the characters other players will have built, and the game you have played is very different than what it would have been had you built your character differently, initially and throughout the game.

A game like *Arcanum* involves playing with identities in a very interesting way. Three different types of identity are at stake. First, there is a *virtual* identity: one's identity as a virtual character in the virtual world of Arcanum. When I played the game, I constructed my character to be a female Half-Elf named "Bead." In the virtual world of Arcanum, given the sort of creature Bead is (a female Half-Elf) and how I have developed her in the game at any one point, there are things she can do and things she cannot do. For example, at a certain point in the game, Bead wanted to persuade a town meeting to fund the building of a monument in order to please the mayor of the town. To do this, she needed to be both intelligent and persuasive. Half-Elves are, by nature, pretty intelligent and I had built up Bead to be persuasive during the game (i.e. by giving her points in this area as she gained more experience). So she was able to pull off the task at the town meeting. Thus these traits (her intelligence and persuasive skills) and her accomplishment at the town meeting – for which she received ample praise – are part of my virtual identity as Bead. In the virtual world of Arcanum I was the Half-Elf Bead.

A second identity that is at stake in playing a game like *Arcanum* is a *real-world identity*: namely, my own identity as "James Paul Gee," a non-virtual person playing a computer game. Of course in the real world I have a good many different non-virtual identities. I am a professor, a linguist, an Anglo-American, a middle-aged Baby Boomer male, a parent, an avid reader, a middle-class person initially raised outside the middle class, a former devoted Catholic, a lover of movies, and so on and so forth through a great many other identities. Any one or more of my real-world identities can be engaged, at one point or another, as I am playing *Arcanum*. For example, which of my real-world identities were at play – positively or negatively – when I got such joy at having Bead pick rich people's pockets? When I chose to be a female Half-Elf in the first place?

A third identity that is at stake in playing a game like *Arcanum* is what I will call a *projective identity*, playing on two senses of the word "project," meaning both "to *project* one's values and desires onto the virtual character" (Bead, in this case) and "seeing the virtual character as one's own *project* in the making, a creature whom I imbue with a certain trajectory through time based on my aspirations for what I want that character to be and become." This is the hardest identity to describe, but the most important one for understanding the power of games like *Arcanum*.

A game like *Arcanum* allows me, the player, certain degrees of freedom (choices) in forming my virtual character and developing her throughout the game. In my projective identity I worry about what sort of "person" I want her to be, and what type of history I want her to have had by the time I am done. I want this person and history to reflect my values – though I have to think reflectively and critically about these, since I have never had to project a Half-Elf onto the world before. At the same time, this person and history I am building also reflect what I have learned from playing the game and being Bead in the land of Arcanum. A good role-playing game makes me think new thoughts about what I value and what I don't.

Let me give an example of what I mean. At one point I had Bead sell a ring a dying old man had given her. I regretted this: it was not, on reflection, the sort of thing I wanted the person I desired Bead to be and become to do (and note, too, that what I want her to be and become is not a clone of myself – in my "real" life I don't pick pockets). It was not an event I wanted her to have in her history – in her trajectory through her virtual life – at the end of the day. So I started the game again. This projected person – the kind of person I want Bead to be, the kind of history I want her to have, the kind of person and history I am trying to build in and through her – is what I mean by a projective identity. There is a certain Bakhtian tension here between what *others* have designed (the people who designed the game and the world of *Arcanum*) and what *I myself* make of that design through projecting my real-world values and aspirations onto its degrees of freedom. The design existed before I played, but it is inert until I vitalize it with new possibilities.

This three-part play of identities involving a virtual identity, real-world identities, and a projective identity is quite powerful. It transcends identification with characters in novels or movies, for instance, because it is both *active* (the player actively does things) and *reflexive*, in the sense that once the player has made some choices about the virtual character, the virtual character is now developed in a way that sets certain parameters about what the player can now do. The virtual character redounds back on the player and affects his or her further actions.

As a player, I was proud of Bead at the end of the game in a way in which I have never been proud of a character in a novel or movie, however much I had identified with them. For a character in a novel or movie, I can identify with the pride they must or should feel, given what they have done or how far they have come. But my pride in Bead is tinged with pride in myself as well (or it could have been regret, had things turned out differently). But this pride is not (just) selfish. In a sense it is also selfless, since it is pride at things that have transcended – taken me outside of – my real-world self (selves), if I am playing the game reflectively.

Of course, from the standpoint of critical theory, one could readily criticize role-playing games like *Arcanum* for essentializing traits like "intelligence" and "strength," or for distributing them differently to different sorts of creatures. It is, of course, not surprising that computer games indulge in the vices of the cultures they inhabit, though they also offer opportunities to reflect on these matters in a novel form. Be that as it may, I will leave cultural critique of computer games to others and to myself for another time.

What I want to concentrate on here is the way in which the three-part play of and with identities I discussed above can illuminate how identity works elsewhere in the contemporary world. In a good science classroom (good by my standards, at least), children are invited to take on the virtual identity of being a scientist of a certain type in words, deeds, and interactions (after all, they are not "really" scientists and are not going to become scientists any time soon – and indeed there are aspects of "real" science and "real" scientists we may not want children imitating). This identity is determined by the values, norms, and design work of the teacher as she or he sets out what constitutes in this classroom being a scientist and doing science.

This virtual identity impinges on and bridges to the real-world identities of different children in the classroom in different ways. Indeed, if children cannot or will not make bridges between some of their real-world identities and the virtual identity at stake in the classroom (here, a particular type of scientist) – or if teachers or others destroy or don't help build such bridges – then, once again, learning is imperiled. Children who, for instance, see themselves as members of families that are adept at technical learning may have an advantage, since they can build a powerful bridge between one of their real-world identities ("people like us learn technical stuff – it's no big deal") and the virtual identity at stake in the science classroom ("scientists in the sort of semiotic domain being created in this classroom do not fear or put off technical learning").

However, active and critical learners can do more than simply carry out the role of playing a virtual scientist in a classroom. They can form a projective identity as well. If learners are to do this, they must come to project their own values and desires onto the virtual identity of "being a scientist of a certain sort" in this classroom. They must, as well, come to see this virtual identity as their own project in the making – an identity they take on that entails a certain trajectory through time defined by their own values, desires, choices, and goals, as these are rooted in the interface of their real-world identities and the virtual identity.

The learners, when they take on a projective identity, want the scientist they are "playing" to be a certain sort of person and to have had a certain sort of history in the learning trajectory of this classroom. They have aspirations for this scientist, just as I had aspirations for Bead when I played *Arcanum*. Perhaps they want *their* scientist to have had a history of having been persistent, resilient in the face of failure, collaborative, risk-taking, skeptical, and creative. They want *their* scientist to become *this* sort of person.

If learners in classrooms carry learning so far as to take on a projective identity, something magic happens – a magic that cannot, in fact, take place in playing a computer game. The learner comes to know that he or she has the *capacity*, at some level, to take on the virtual identity as a real-world identity. However much I might want to, I myself, in the real world, have no capacity to become the sort of female Half-Elf I wanted and built Bead to be. But a learner in a good science classroom comes to feel what it is like to have the capacity to be the sort of scientist (and person) they have wanted and built their "character" in the classroom to be. This becomes one of their real-world identities.

Learners do not, of course, have to realize this capacity in actuality and become a scientist. They don't even have to feel they could become particularly good scientists – after all, in the projective identity you also learn about your own limitations. It is often enough that they have sensed new powers in themselves. They will, possibly for a lifetime, be able to empathize with, affiliate with, learn more about, and even critique science as a valued, but vulnerable, human enterprise.

Thus what *others* have designed (a virtual world in a game or classroom) becomes part of myself, my real-world identity – my own uniqueness – when and if I engage in the virtual identity as a project of my own, and not just a role to be played by the rules of the game/classroom (for a win or a grade). My projective identity stands at the border of the social (the virtual world created by others) and myself (my real-world identities, which themselves are the products of my own past projective work). The social and the individual are inextricably linked.

Of course such projective identities are often worked out much more creatively in playing computer games than in studying in classrooms, especially classrooms that stress skill-and-drill, the passive storage of information, and standards that the learner has had no part in forming. In such classrooms there are no degrees of freedom for the projective identity to take wing. As young people face the contemporary demand to be shaping-shifting portfolio people, the sort of play with identity that is characteristic of contemporary forms like video and computer games will be practiced by some more than others, more in some schools than others, and sometimes more outside school than in it. Indeed, access to these technologies themselves will be greater for some than for others (and, thus far, they are recruited little or not at all by schools). What if projective identities turn out to be a central form of learning for our "new times"? What if they turn out to be a key site at which the Bakhtian tension between the social/cultural/historical and the individual works itself out in the modern world? I can offer the questions. I have no firm answers.

8

A FINAL WORD
The content fetish

Throughout this book I have stated principles that any good learning environment, whether inside or outside school, ought to have. If the reader wants "practical" recommendations, then the best thing to do is to ask how these principles could be differently implemented in different types of learning settings. And of course there would have to be differences in implementation, since each learning situation is different and calls for customized implementations not general ones. If I wanted to offer a "reader's exercise," I would suggest that readers go through the book, underline principles of good learning and state for themselves how they could be implemented in the specific learning situations they care about.

But the bottom line is this: if any variety of language is to be learned and used, it has to be *situated*. That is, it has to be brought down to concrete exemplifications in experiences learners have had (repeatedly, since learning is partly a practice effect). These experiences need to be guided by "masters" (whether teachers or not), so that learners pay attention to the right things amidst the myriad flux of any experience and form good and useful generalizations. "Useful generalizations" here does not mean "general truths"; rather it means that the learners can form mental simulations based on their experiences – simulations that are useful for guiding future thought and action in the world, both individually and collaboratively.

There is one major barrier in schools to implementing the sort of perspective on language and learning discussed in this book. This is what I call the "content fetish." When people think of learning in school, they almost always define it around "content": that is, in terms of the facts and principles germane to a given academic domain like biology, history, social studies, and so forth. They ask, first and foremost, "What facts and principles – that is, what information – in this domain do I want learners to know?" And then they go on from this point to build their learning environment.

But academic domains – the so-called "content" areas of school – are, out in the world, not first and foremost "bodies of information." Rather they are things people do with – if you like, they are games people play with – those bodies of information and the various sorts of tools and technologies associated with them.

Biologists know how to do certain things with the information and tools they have. Furthermore, good biologists know how to do good things with some information and tools in biology, but not all information and tools in biology. There are always parts of biology they don't know or now don't remember.

I once saw, in a lecture to a bunch of undergraduates, one of the world's top geneticists forget Mendel's laws (something any freshman biology student knows). He stopped, manipulated a few symbols on the blackboard and recreated the laws on the spot, then went on. He had symbolic tools to recover the laws. That was what made him smart, not that he had memorized some facts. He had picked up these tools by doing things – playing certain games with symbols and the world – not by memorizing facts out of context.

One implication that I hope this book has is this: if you want to design a learning environment, don't start with content, start with the following sorts of questions: "What experiences do I want the learners to have? What simulations do I want them to able to build in their heads? What do I want them to be able to do? What information, tools, and technologies do they need?" Another way to put these questions is: "What games do I want these learners to be able to play?" The first decision, then, ought to be about what are good and useful and powerful experiences for people to have, and what are good and useful and powerful games for them to be able to play.

If one thinks hard about these matters, sometimes the answers are academic in the sense that the experiences and games are ones we associate with academic domains. Sometimes they are not. It is no longer useful to cut up the world the way Aristotle did in terms of our traditional academic disciplines seen as bodies of facts and information. We need to start cutting up the world in terms of what constitutes good games for thinking about and, ultimately, making better worlds for everyone. In those terms, Mendel's laws make for some very good games. So does Pokémon. In fact, both Mendel's laws and Pokémon have to do with the nearly limitless variety that can flow from a rather simple, but elegant, set of underlying characteristics. Let's remember that Mendel failed his school-based fact-packed exam to become a high-school biology teacher. That's why he was playing around in the monastery garden with pea plants inventing modern genetics and in the act rewriting all future biology textbooks.

REFERENCES

Abrams, M. H. (1953). *The mirror and the lamp: Romantic theory and the critical tradition.* Oxford: Oxford University Press.

Adams, M. J. (1990). *Beginning to read: Thinking and learning about print.* Cambridge, MA: MIT Press.

Aronson, E. (1978). *The jigsaw classroom.* Beverly Hills, CA: Sage.

Baker, S. K., Simmons, D. C., and Kameenui, E. J. (n.d.). Vocabulary acquisition: Synthesis of the research: http://idea.uoregon.edu/~ncite/documents/techrep/tech13.html.

Beck, I. and McKeown, M. (1991). Conditions of vocabulary acquisition. In R. Barr, M. Kamil, P. Mosenthal, and P. D. Pearson, eds, *Handbook of reading research,* vol. 2. New York: Longman, pp. 789–814.

Bakhtin, M. M. (1981). *The dialogic imagination.* Austin: University of Texas Press.

Bakhtin, M. M. (1986). *Speech genres and other late essays.* Austin: University of Texas Press.

Barsalou, L. W. (1999a). Language comprehension: Archival memory or preparation for situated action. *Discourse Processes* 28: 61–80.

Barsalou, L. W. (1999b). Perceptual symbol systems. *Behavioral and Brain Sciences* 22: 577–660.

Barton, D. (1994). *Literacy: An introduction to the ecology of written language.* Oxford: Blackwell.

Bauman, Z. (1992). *Intimations of postmodernity.* London: Routledge.

Bauman, Z. (1998). *Globalization: The human consequences.* Cambridge: Polity Press.

Beck, U. (1999). *World risk society.* Oxford: Blackwell.

Beck, U. (2000). *The brave new world of work.* Cambridge: Polity Press.

Beck, U., Giddens, A., and Lash, S. (1994). *Reflexive modernization: Politics, traditions and aesthetics in the modern social order.* Stanford, CA: Stanford University Press.

Bereiter, C. and Scardamalia, M. (1993). *Surpassing ourselves: An inquiry into the nature and implications of expertise.* Chicago: Open Court.

Berger, P., Berger, B., and Kellner, H. (1973). *The homeless mind: Modernization and consciousness.* New York: Random House.

Boyett, J. H. and Conn, H. P. (1992). *Workplace 2000: The revolution reshaping American business.* New York: Plume/Penguin.

Bransford, J. D. and Schwartz, D. L. (1999). Rethinking transfer: A simple proposal with multiple implications. *Review of Research in Education* 24: 61–100.

Brown, A. L. (1994). The advancement of learning. *Educational Researcher* 23: 4–12.

Brown, A. L., Collins, A., and Dugid, P. (1989). Situated cognition and the culture of learning. *Educational Researcher* 18: 32–42.

119

Carnine, D. W., Silbert, J., and Kameenui, E. J. (1996). *Direct instruction reading*, 3rd edition. Englewood Cliffs, NJ: Prentice-Hall.

Castells, M. (1996). *The information age: Economy, society, and culture*, vol. 1: *The rise of the network society*. Oxford: Blackwell.

Cazden, C. B. (1972). *Child language and education*. New York: Holt, Rinehart and Winston.

Chall, J. S., Jacobs, V., and Baldwin, L. (1990). *The reading crisis: Why poor children fall behind*. Cambridge, MA: Harvard University Press.

Chaney, C. (1992). Language development, metalinguistic skills, and print awareness in 3–year-old children. *Applied Psycholinguistics* 13: 485–99.

Chomsky, N. (1965). *Cartesian linguistics*. New York: Harper and Row, 1965. Reprinted as *Cartesian linguistics. A chapter in the history of Rationalist thought*. Lanham, MD: University Press of America, 1986.

Chomsky, N. (1968). *Language and mind*. New York: Harcourt Brace & World, Inc., Reprinted enlarged edition, New York: Harcourt Brace Jovanovich, 1972.

Chomsky, N. (1986). *Knowledge of language: Its nature, origin, and use*. New York: Praeger.

Chomsky, N. (1995). *The minimalist program*. Cambridge, MA: MIT Press.

Christe, F., ed. (1990). *Literacy for a changing world*. Melbourne: Australian Council for Educational Research.

Clark, A. (1997). *Being there: Putting brain, body, and world together again*. Cambridge, MA: MIT Press.

Clark, A. (2003). *Natural-born cyborgs: Why minds and technologies are made to merge*. Oxford: Oxford University Press.

Coles, G. (1998). *Reading lessons: The debate over literacy*. New York: Hill and Wang.

Coles, G. (2000). *Misreading reading: The bad science that hurts children*. Portsmouth, NH: Heinemann.

Coles, G. (2003). *Reading the naked truth: Literacy, legislation, and lies*. Portsmouth, NH: Heinemann.

Cope, B. and Kalantzis, M., eds (1993). *The powers of literacy: A genre approach to teaching writing*. Pittsburgh, PA: University of Pittsburgh Press.

Damon, W. (1983). *Social and personality development*. New York: Norton.

Dennett, D. C. (1969). *Content and consciousness*. London: Routledge.

diSessa, A. A. (2000). *Changing minds: Computers, learning, and literacy*. Cambridge, MA: MIT Press.

Drucker, P. F. (1989). *The new realities: In government and politics, in economics and business, in society and world view*. New York: HarperCollins.

Drucker, P. F. (1999). *Management challenges for the 21st century*. New York: Harper.

D'Souza, D. (2001). *Virtue of prosperity: Finding values in an age of techno-affluence*. New York: Touchstone Books.

Dunn, J. (1988). *The beginnings of social understanding*. Oxford: Blackwell.

Edelsky, C. (1994). *With literacy and justice for all: Rethinking the social in language and education*, 2nd edition. London: Taylor & Francis.

Elley, R. (1992). *How in the world do students read?* Hamburg: The Hague International Association for the Evaluation of Educational Achievement.

Engestrom, Y., Miettinen, R., and Punamaki, R. L., eds (1999). *Perspectives on activity theory*. Cambridge: Cambridge University Press.

Fausto-Sterling, A. (1985). *Myths of gender: Biological theories about women and men*. New York: Basic Books.

Ferguson, R. F. (1998). Teacher's perceptions and expectations and the Black–White test score gap. In C. Jencks and M. Phillips, eds, *The Black–White test score gap*. Washington, DC: Brookings Institution Press, pp. 273–317.

Finn, P. J. (1999). *Literacy with an attitude: Educating working-class children in their own self-interest.* Albany, NY: State University of New York Press.

Foley, M. and Ratner, H. (1997). Children's recoding in memory for collaboration: A way of learning from others. *Cognitive Development* 13: 91–108.

Frank, J. (1963). Spatial form in modern literature. In *The widening gyre: Crisis and mastery in modern literature*. Bloomington, IN: Indiana University Press, pp. 3–62.

Frank, R. H. and Cook, P. J. (1995). *The winner-take-all society: How more and more Americans compete for ever fewer and bigger prizes, encouraging economic waste, income inequality, and an impoverished cultural life*. New York: The Free Press.

Freedman, S. W., Simons, E. R., Kalnin, J. S., Casareno, A., and the M-Class Teams (1999). *Inside city schools: Investigating literacy in multicultural classrooms*. New York: Teachers College Press.

Gee, J. P. (1990). *Social linguistics and literacies: Ideology in discourses*. London: Taylor & Francis.

Gee, J. P. (1992). *The social mind: Language, ideology, and social practice*. New York: Bergin & Garvey.

Gee, J. P. (1996). *Social linguistics and literacies: Ideology in discourses*, 2nd edition. London: Routledge/Taylor & Francis.

Gee, J. P. (1999a). *An introduction to discourse analysis: Theory and method*. London: Routledge.

Gee, J. P. (1999b). New people in new worlds: Networks, the new capitalism and schools. In B. Cope and M. Kalantzis, eds, *Multiliteracies: Literacy learning and the design of social futures*. London: Routledge, 1999, pp. 43–68.

Gee, J. P. (2000). Teenagers in new times: A new literacy studies perspective. *Journal of Adolescent & Adult Literacy* 43.5: 412–20.

Gee, J. P. (2000–1). Identity as an analytic lens for research in education. *Review of Research in Education* 25: 99–125.

Gee, J. P. (2001). Progressivism, critique, and socially situated minds. In C. Dudley-Marling and C. Edelsky, eds, *The fate of progressive language policies and practices*. Urbana, IL: NCTE, pp. 31–58.

Gee, J. P. (2002). Literacies, identities, and discourses. In M. Schleppegrel and M. Cecilia Colombi, eds, *Developing advanced literacy in first and second languages: Meaning with power*, Mahwah, NJ: Lawrence Erlbaum, pp. 159–75.

Gee, J. P. (2003). *What video games have to teach us about learning and literacy*. New York: Palgrave/Macmillan.

Gee, J. P. and Crawford, V. (1998). Two kinds of teenagers: Language, identity, and social class. In D. Alverman, K. Hinchman, D. Moore, S. Phelps, and D. Waff, eds, *Reconceptualizing the literacies in adolescents' lives*. Hillsdale, NJ: Erlbaum, pp. 225–45.

Gee, J. P., Hull, G., and Lankshear, C. (1996). *The new work order: Behind the language of the new capitalism*. Boulder, CO: Westview.

Gee, J. P., Allen, A.-R., and Clinton, K. (2001). Language, class, and identity: Teenagers fashioning themselves through language. *Linguistics and Education* 12: 175–94.

Gersten, R., Fuchs, L. S., Williams, J. P., and Baker, S. (2001). Teaching reading comprehension strategies to students with learning disabilities: A review of research. *Review of Educational Research* 71: 279–320.

Gilbert, R. and Gilbert, P. (1998). *Masculinity goes to school*. London: Routledge.

Gladwell, M. (2000). *The tipping point: How little things can make a big difference*. Boston, MA: Little, Brown and Company.

Glenberg, A. M. (1997). What is memory for? *Behavioral and Brain Sciences* 20: 1–55.

Glenberg, A. M. and Robertson, D. A. (1999). Indexical understanding of instructions. *Discourse Processes* 28: 1–26.

Goldberg, K., ed. (2001). *The robot in the garden: Telerobotics and telepistemology in the age of the Internet*. Cambridge, MA: MIT Press.

Goodman, K. (1998). *In defense of good teaching: What teachers need to know about the "reading wars"*. Portland, ME: Stenhouse.

Goody, J. (1977). *The domestication of the savage mind*. Cambridge: Cambridge University Press.

Goody, J. and Watt, I. P. (1963). The consequences of literacy. *Comparative Studies in History and Society*, 5: 304–45.

Goto, S. (2003). Basic writing and policy reform: Why we keep talking past each other. *Journal of Basic Writing* 21: 16–32.

Gould, S. J. (1981). *The mismeasure of man*. New York: Norton.

Greenfield, P. M. (1984). *Mind and media: The effects of television, video games, and computers*. Cambridge, MA: Harvard University Press.

Greider, W. (1997). *One world, ready or not: The manic logic of global capitalism*. New York: Simon & Schuster.

Grissmer, D., Flanagan, A., and Williamson, S. (1998). Why did the Black–White score gap narrow in the 1970s and 1980s? In C. Jencks and M. Phillips, eds, *The Black–White test score gap*. Washington, DC: Brookings Institution Press, pp. 182–226.

Halliday, M. A. K. and Martin, J. R. (1993). *Writing science: Literacy and discursive power*. Pittsburgh: University of Pittsburgh Press.

Handy, C. (1989). *The age of unreason*. London: Business Books.

Hanks, W. F. (1996). *Language and communicative practices*. Boulder, CO: Westview Press.

Hayek, F. A. (1996). *Individualism and economic order*, reissue edition. Chicago: University of Chicago Press.

Hedges, L. V. and Nowell, A. (1998). Black–White test score convergence since 1965. In C. Jencks and M. Phillips, eds, *The Black–White test score gap*. Washington, DC: Brookings Institution Press, pp. 149–81.

Holland, D. and Quinn, N., eds (1987). *Cultural models in language and thought*. Cambridge: Cambridge University Press.

Hollinger, E. M. and Ratkos, J. M. (1999). *Pokemon: Gotta catch 'em all! Prima's official strategy guide*. Rocklin, CA: Prima Games.

Howe, N. and Strauss, W. (2000). *Millennials rising: The next great generation*. New York: Vintage Books.

Hutchins, E. (1995). *Cognition in the wild*. Cambridge, MA: MIT Press.

Jencks, C. and Phillips, M., eds (1998). *The Black–White test score gap*. Washington, DC: Brookings Institution Press.

Kanigel, R. (1997). *The one best way: Frederick Winslow Taylor and the enigma of efficiency*. New York: Penguin.

Kelly, A. E., ed. (2003). Theme issue: The role of design in educational research. *Educational Researcher* 32: 3–37.

Kelly, K. (1998). *New rules for the new economy: Ten radical strategies for a connected world*. New York: Viking.

Kirshner, D. and Whitson, J. A., eds (1997). *Situated cognition: Social, semiotic, and psychological perspectives*. Norwood, NJ: Lawrence Erlbaum.

Kress, G. and Van Leeuwen, T. (2001). *Multimodal discourse: The modes and media of contemporary communication*. London: Arnold.

REFERENCES

Kress G., Jewitt, C., Ogborn, J., and Tsatsarelis, C. (2001). *Multimodal teaching and learning: The rhetorics of the science classroom.* London: Continuum.

Kruger, A. (1992). The effect of peer and adult–child transactive discussions on moral reasoning. *Merrill-Palmer Quarterly* 38: 191–211.

Kruger, A. and Tomasello, M. (1986). Transactive discussions with peers and adults. *Developmental Psychology* 22: 681–5.

Labov, W. (1972). *Language in the inner city.* Philadelphia, PA: University of Pennsylvania Press.

Labov, W. and Waletsky, J. (1967). Narrative analysis: Oral versions of personal experience. In J. Helm, ed., *Essays on the verbal and visual arts.* Seattle: University of Washington Press, pp. 12–44.

Lam, W. S. E. (2000). L2 literacy and the design of the self: A case study of a teenager writing on the Internet. *TESOL Quarterly* 34.3: 457–82.

Latour, B. (1999). *Pandora's hope: Essays on the reality of science studies.* Cambridge, MA: Harvard University Press.

Lave, J. (1996). Teaching, as learning, in practice. *Mind, Culture, and Activity* 3: 149–64.

Lave, J. and Wenger, E. (1991). *Situated learning: Legitimate peripheral participation.* New York: Cambridge University Press.

Liberman, I. and Liberman, A. (1990). Whole language vs. code emphasis: Underlying assumptions and their implications for reading instruction. *Annals of Dyslexia* 40: 51–76.

Lyon, G. R. (1998). Overview of reading and literacy research. In S. Patton and M. Holmes, eds, *The keys to literacy.* Washington, DC: Council for Basic Education, pp. 1–15.

Martin, J. R. (1990). Literacy in science: Learning to handle text as technology. In F. Christe, ed., *Literacy for a changing world.* Melbourne: Australian Council for Educational Research, pp. 79–117.

National Assessment of Educational Progress (1997). *NAEP 1996 trends in academic progress.* Washington, DC: US Government Printing Office.

National Institute of Child Health and Human Development (2000a). *Report of the National Reading Panel. Teaching children to read: An evidence-based assessment of the scientific research literature on reading and its implications for reading instruction* (NIH Publication No. 00-4769). Washington, DC: US Government Printing Office.

National Institute of Child Health and Human Development (2000b). *Report of the National Reading Panel. Teaching children to read: An evidence-based assessment of the scientific research literature on reading and its implications for reading instruction: Reports of the subgroups* (NIH Publication No. 00-4754). Washington, DC: US Government Printing Office.

Neisser, U., ed. (1998). *The rising curve: Long-term gains in IQ and related measures.* Washington, DC: American Psychological Association.

New London Group (1996). A pedagogy of multiliteracies: Designing social futures. *Harvard Educational Review* 66: 60–92. Reprinted in B. Cope and M. Kalantzis, eds (1999). *Multiliteracies: Literacy learning and the design of social futures.* London: Routledge, pp. 9–37.

Olson, D. R. (1977). From utterance to text: The bias of language in speech and writing. *Harvard Education Review* 47: 257–81.

Olson, D. R. (1994). *The world on paper: The conceptual and cognitive implications of writing and reading.* Cambridge: Cambridge University Press.

Ong, W. J. (1982). *Orality and literacy: The technologizing of the word.* London: Methuen.

123

O'Reilly, B. (2000). Meet the future – It's your kids. *Fortune*, 24 July 2000, pp. 144–68.

Peters, T. (1987). *Thriving on chaos: A handbook for management revolution*. New York: Harper & Row.

Piaget, J. (1932). *The moral judgment of the child*. London: Kegan Paul.

Pinker, S. (1994). *The language instinct: How the mind creates language*. New York: William Marrow.

Poole, S. (2000). *Trigger happy: Videogames and the entertainment revolution*. New York: Arcade Publishing.

Public Agenda (1997). *Getting by: What American teenagers really think about their schools*. New York: Public Agenda.

Rayner, K., Foorman, B. R., Perfetti, E., Pesetsky, D., and Seidenberg, M. S. (2001). How psychological science informs the teaching of reading. In *Psychological science in the public interest*, monograph 2. Washington, DC: American Psychological Society, pp. 31–74.

Rayner, K., Foorman, B. R., Perfetti, C. A., Pesetsky, D., and Seidenberg, M. S. (2002). How should reading be taught? *Scientific American* March: 84–91.

Reich, R. B. (1992). *The work of nations*. New York: Vintage Books.

Rifkin, J. (1995). *The end of work: The decline of the global labor market and the dawn of the post-market era*. New York: Jeremy P. Tarcher.

Rifkin, J. (2000). *The age of access: The new culture of hypercapitalism where all of life is a paid-for experience*. New York: Jeremy Tarcher/Putnam.

Rogoff, B. (1990). *Apprenticeship in thinking: Cognitive development in social context*. New York: Oxford University Press.

Rose, F. (1997). Toward a class-cultural theory of social movements: Reinterpreting new social movements. *Sociological Forum* 12.3: 461–93.

Rose. M. (1999). *Possible lives: The promise of public education in America*. New York, Penguin.

Schleppegrell, M. (2004). *Language of schooling: A functional linguistics perspective*. Mahwah, NJ: Lawrence Erlbaum.

Schleppegrel, M. and Cecilia Colombi, M., eds (2002). *Developing advanced literacy in first and second languages: Meaning with power*. Mahwah, NJ: Lawrence Erlbaum, pp. 159–75.

Scollon, R. and Scollon, S. B. K. (1981). *Narrative, literacy, and face in interethnic communication*. Norwood, NJ: Ablex.

Smith, H. (1995). *Rethinking America: A new game plan from American innovators: Schools, business, people, work*. New York: Random House.

Snow, C. (1986). Conversations with children. In P. Fletcher and M. Garman, eds, *Language acquisition*, 2nd edition. Cambridge: Cambridge University Press, pp. 69–89.

Snow, C. E., Burns, M. S., and Griffin, P., eds (1998). *Preventing reading difficulties in young children*. Washington, DC: National Academy Press.

Steele, C. M. (1992). Race and the schooling of Black America. *Atlantic Monthly* April: 68–78.

Steele, C. M. and Aronson, J. (1995). A threat in the air: How stereotypes shape the intellectual identities and performance of women and African Americans. *Journal of Personality and Social Psychology* 69.5: 797–811.

Steele, C. M. and Aronson, J. (1998). Stereotype threat and the test performance of academically successful African Americans. In C. Jencks and M. Phillips, eds, *The Black–White test score gap*. Washington, DC: Brookings Institution Press, pp. 401–27.

Sowell, T. (1996). *The vision of the anointed: Self-congratulation as a basis for social policy*. New York: Basic Books.

REFERENCES

Street, B. (1995). *Social literacies: Critical approaches to literacy in development, ethnography and education*. London: Longman.

Thurow, L. C. (1999). *Building wealth: The new rules for individuals, companies, and nations in a knowledge-based economy*. New York: HarperCollins.

Tomasello, M. (1999). *The cultural origins of human cognition*. Cambridge, MA: Harvard University Press.

von Mises, L. (1997). *Human action: A treatise on economics*, 4th revised edition. San Francisco: Fox & Wilkes.

Vygotsky, L. S. (1978). *Mind in society: The development of higher psychological processes*. Cambridge, MA: Harvard University Press.

Wenger, E. (1998). *Communities of practice: Learning, meaning, and identity*. Cambridge: Cambridge University Press.

Wenger, E., McDermott, R., and Snyder, W. M. (2002). *Cultivating communities of practice*. Cambridge, MA: Harvard Business School Press.

Wertsch, J. V. (1998). *Mind as action*. Oxford: Oxford University Press.

Wittgenstein, L. (1958). *Philosophical investigations*, trans. G. E. M. Anscombe. Oxford: Basil Blackwell.

INDEX

Note: page numbers in **bold** indicate boxes and tables.

Related titles from Routledge

An Introduction to Discourse Analysis
Theory and Method

James Paul Gee

'If you only read one book on discourse analysis, this is the one to read. Gee shows us that discourse analysis is about a lot more than linguistic study; it's about how to keep from, as he says, 'getting physically, socially, culturally, or morally "bitten" by the world'.'

Ron Scollon, *Georgetown University, USA*

James Paul Gee presents here his unique integrated approach to discourse analysis: the analysis of spoken and written language as it is used to enact social and cultural perspectives and identities.

Assuming no prior knowledge of linguistics, the book presents both a theory of language-in-use, as well as a method of research. This method is made up of 'tools of inquiry' and strategies for using them.

Perspectives from a variety of approaches and disciplines, including applied linguistics, education, psychology, anthropology, and communication, are incorporated to help students and scholars from a range of backgrounds formulate their own views and engage in their own discourse analyses.

0–415–21186–7 (hbk)
0–415–21185–9 (pbk)

Available at all good bookshops

For ordering and further information please visit:
www.routledge.com

Related titles from Routledge

Literacy in the New Media Age
Literacies

Gunther Kress

'In his new book, Gunther Kress shows us that as reading and writing move from page to screen, we must understand literacy not just as a matter of language but also as motivated multimedia design'

Jay L. Lemke, *City University of New York, USA*

In this 'new media age' the screen has replaced the book as the dominant medium. At the same time image is displacing writing and moving into the centre of communication.

In this ground-breaking new book, Gunther Kress considers the effects of this revolution and, taking into account social, economic, communicational and technological factors, provides a framework of principles for understanding these changes and their effects on the future of literacy. He argues that the move to screen will produce far-reaching shifts in relations of power and explores the democratic potentials and effects of the new information and communication techonologies.

Literacy in the New Media Age is essential reading for anyone with an interest in literacy and its wider political and cultural implications.

0–415–25355–1 (hbk)
0–415–25356–X (pbk)

Available at all good bookshops

For ordering and further information please visit:
www.routledge.com/rcenters/linguistics/series/literacies